Love in Twelfth-Century France

Love

in

Twelfth-Century France

John C. Moore

UNIVERSITY OF PENNSYLVANIA PRESS
PHILADELPHIA

Stanzas from *Medieval Epics,* ed. Angel Flores (New York: Dell, 1963) on pp. 84–85, 87–89, 99, 100, 121, reproduced by permission of the editor. Stanzas from *Medieval Latin Lyrics,* trans. Helen Waddell (London: Constable, 5th ed., 1948), on pp. 121–22, 155, reproduced by permission of the publishers.

for

FATHER JOSEPH A. MCCALLIN, S.J.

Patri meo in Spiritu

Preface

This book is intended for the student and the general reader, but I hope that some scholars too may find it useful. Outside of our own areas of specialization, many of us become "general readers" seeking easy access to complicated bodies of knowledge. All are welcome here.

A few technical points for the scholarly reader. Translations are my own unless otherwise indicated. Biblical quotations are from the Revised Standard Version, although I have modified the translation in a number of instances to bring it closer to the Vulgate. Throughout, I've quoted translations I thought readable and cited editions I thought accessible. PL is an abbreviation for *Patrologia Latina,* ed. J. P. Migne, 221 vols. (Paris, 1844–55); RHGF is an abbreviation for *Recueil des historiens des Gaules et de la France,* 24 vols. (Paris, 1737–1904).

I wish to express my thanks to all those who, in one way or another, made this book possible: The Frank L. Weil Institute for Studies in Religion and the Humanities; Professor Benjamin Nelson; my colleagues at Hofstra University, particularly Linton S. Thorn, John T. Marcus, and the late Gerrit P. Judd; and finally my wife, Patricia, who has been my fellow-student of love for some years now.

J.C.M.

Contents

Illustrations

CHAPTER ONE:

Introduction

"GREAT IS the force of love, wondrous is its strength. Many are the degrees of love, and great the differences among them. And who can worthily distinguish among them or even enumerate them?" So speaks Richard of St. Victor, a twelfth-century cleric.[1] Whatever love is, it has aroused the curiosity of the men and women of Western civilization as has no other subject. Love is something people do or enjoy, something that happens to them, something they fall into. It is something people think about. Literature, art, and music are filled with themes of love. Psychiatrists, theologians, poets, scientists, nearly all have said that love is something good and necessary. But ancients and moderns alike have failed to agree about what love really is.

The disagreement is not surprising. Like truth and beauty, love is one of the great intangibles. It cannot be

I

measured, weighed, or analyzed into its chemical components. It reveals nothing in a spectrograph. But it is surprising that Western civilization, proud of its tradition of lucid rationality, has continued to tolerate a really deplorable laxity in the use of the term *love.* Today a man can "love" his God, his country, his mother, his father, his wife, his work, his children, his neighbor's wife, his sports car, his dog, and his bourbon. Some of these are expected to "love" him in return. The poverty of the English language seems to impose an impossible burden upon one little, four-letter "Anglo-Saxon" word—a word of a kind usually noted for precision if not for delicacy.

Unfortunately, the languages of twelfth-century France were no better. Unlike the educated American, the educated Frenchman of the twelfth century had at least two languages at his disposal, Latin and French. Twelfth-century writers learned their Latin from the pagan and Christian writers of ancient Rome and from the Vulgate Bible. There they found the nouns *amor, dilectio,* and *caritas* and the verbs *amare* and *diligere,* all meaning *love.* From these Latin words were derived the French *amour* (and its variants) and *charité.* One might have hoped that with these rich resources, twelfth-century writers would have cleared things up a little by carefully reserving each word for a certain kind of love. Unhappily, they did not. True, the Latin *caritas* was used only for a good love, usually Christian in character. True, the French *charité* had a similar usage, though it was already taking on the meaning of "charitable" service, alms-giving and the like. But *amor, dilectio,* and *amour* could be used indiscriminately, for the love of God and of mammon alike.[2] A twelfth-century viscountess was said to have commented that the love between man and wife and the love between lovers were two entirely different things and that "the ambiguous nature of the word" prevented their comparison.[3] Ambiguous it was then, and ambiguous it has remained.

Still, twelfth-century France has a special attraction for the historian of love. Love then occupied the attention of thoughtful and creative men and women as it did in no other medieval century. Twelfth-century France was the scene of St. Bernard's mystic love of God, of the tragic love affair of Heloise and Abelard, and of the new "romantic" love of troubadours and writers of romances. Consequently, the subject has richness and variety. At the same time, it is contained within manageable limits of time and space.

The twelfth century was one of energy, growth, and ambition for all of Europe. As the century opened, Christendom was still exhilarated with the success of the knights of France in the first crusade. In 1099, they had knelt in the blood of massacred Saracens and wept for joy. Jerusalem was theirs. Only a few years before, the men of Genoa and Pisa had driven the Moslems from Sardinia, and knights from Norman France had taken Sicily from the Moslems. Similarly, in Spain the frontiers of Islam were being pushed southward by Christian knights. Throughout the century, the sons and grandsons of the first crusaders came and went

3

France in the Twelfth Century. Map by Linton S. Thorn.

between Europe and the Holy Land, and in their wake followed merchants and pilgrims. Within Europe, the "medieval boom" was well under way with a growing population, increased agricultural production, and expanding commerce. Forests were being cleared and swamps drained to make way for new farm land. Settlers in these new lands founded the "new towns" of Europe: Villeneuve, Villanova, Neuburg. Technological innovations, like heavy, wheeled plows and watermills, made the labor of peasant farmers more fruitful, and nearly everyone profited from the increased wealth. Growing numbers of craftsmen and merchants were building cities, travelling the roads, and sailing the seas and rivers. A new society was developing, rooted in the rich resources of Europe, in new techniques for exploiting those resources, and in the organizing skills of medieval princes, clergy, and townsmen. The foundations of modern Europe were being laid.

"France" participated in these changes, but not in the sense that France was a clearly defined unit. In the twelfth century, it had neither today's internal unity nor today's sharp differences from neighboring areas. The kings of France claimed authority over an area almost equal to modern France, with the eastern boundary running from north to south, roughly along the Scheldt or Escaut, the upper Meuse, the Saône, and the Rhone. In practice, however, the king had no control over most of this kingdom. Chroniclers frequently called it "Gaul" and reserved the name "France" for the area around Paris. Besides political divisions, the kingdom was also divided by sharp cultural differences, especially between north and south. The southern part spoke a dialect which gave the area its name, Languedoc, and it breathed the warm air of the Mediterranean. The north, the land of *langue d'oïl,* looked to the Channel and the North Sea. The difference in language, climate, and culture made Languedoc seem like foreign parts to a northerner. In mid-twelfth century, St. Bernard of Clairvaux could say of a heretic fled to the south that he had been "chased from France," so remote seemed Languedoc.[4]

The modern frontiers between France and her neighbors were anticipated in the twelfth century only by ill-defined zones. The pilgrim travelling from northern France to the shrine of St. James of Compostella in Spain would find the differences between Spain and southern France scarcely greater than the differences between the north and south of France itself. Visiting the tomb of St. Thomas Becket in England, he would find a kingdom ruled by a French prince, Henry II, and by a French aristocracy. To the east, the difference between French- and German-speaking peoples was already pronounced, but even here the frontier was not clear and was ignored by French and German nobles as they formed marital and feudal ties.

The weakness of the kings of France means that there is no central government to give focus to the story of twelfth-century France. In 1100, Philip I could scarcely control the vicinity of Paris. His son Louis VI, wrote a chronicler, "suffered many things from the princes of France . . . who refused to do homage to him as was owing."⁵ By 1200, Louis VI's grandson Philip II was much more powerful, but it was still not yet clear that he was stronger than the other great princes of "Gaul." In France, as elsewhere, the nobles were engaged in a struggle first for survival, and then for wealth and power. They nibbled at their neighbors' lands; they formed sworn alliances with one neighbor to despoil another; they married their children hither and yon in elaborate gambles, hoping that the right pattern of births and deaths would bring several principalities into the lap of one of their descendants. The scope of this dynastic lottery can be suggested by the family relationships of Louis VII. His first wife was Eleanor, heiress of Aquitaine, who later married Henry II of England. The two daughters of his first marriage married the counts of Champagne and Blois. Louis VII then married the daughter of the king of Castile and again had two daughters. One married the count of Ponthieu, the other married first Henry the Younger, son of Henry II and Eleanor, and then the king of Hungary. Louis VII's third wife bore him the future King Philip Augustus and a daughter who married the Byzantine emperor in Constantinople. The actual political results of these marriages are a tangle; the possible results are beyond imagining.

Despite the divisions and complications, though, France did develop some political unity. By the end of the century, the Capetian king of France was on the verge of becoming the strongest ruler in Europe. Even more impressive, though, was the cultural preeminence France enjoyed in Europe.

Around 1100, a poet in the north of France composed the *Song of Roland,* a heroic epic which embodied the ideals of the warriors of French courts, and transmitted them beyond the frontiers of France and, indeed, beyond the frontiers of the twelfth century. About the same time, in the south, Duke William IX of Aquitaine was composing the first known troubadour poetry, lyric love poems that were studied works of art. About mid-century, the northern and southern traditions merged. The result was the romance, the eclectic product of the heroic *chansons de geste,* of the artful songs of the troubadours, and of the increasingly leisurely and sophisticated courts which patronized the writers. Around 1170, the poet Chrétien de Troyes boasted that chivalry and learning, having deserted Greece and Rome, had come to dwell in France.[6] The boast still stands; in France, in the twelfth century, modern European literature was born.

Although the religious houses and the schools of France did not set European styles with quite the same unquestioned supremacy as the aristocratic courts, France was still the intellectual and religious heart of Europe. In 1131, when Pope Innocent II consecrated a new abbot at the abbey of Morigni in northern France, two men among the onlookers already surpassed the pope himself in fame, Bernard of Clairvaux and Peter Abelard.[7]

Bernard was the best-known representative of the religious revival already under way in Europe, but he was only one among many. The Burgundian monastery of Cluny, founded in 910, had been the first of the great reforming monasteries, but by 1100 Cluny was old—too old, some thought, too comfortable. Some of those who thought so became hermits, living completely alone or in communities, such as that of Chartreuse, founded in 1084. Others founded new monasteries where the rule of St. Benedict was enforced with greater rigor: Chaise-Dieu, Tiron, and Cîteaux. When Bernard went to Cîteaux in 1112, it was only one small community of monks. When he died in 1153, Cîteaux had about 350 daughter houses, including Bernard's abbey of Clairvaux, and there were over 700 monks at Clairvaux alone. Bernard's contemporary, Peter the Venerable, abbot of Cluny, wrote, "What an innumerable crowd of monks has divine grace provided in our day! It has covered almost all the fields of Gaul; it has filled the towns, the castles, and the fortified places! How varied in custom and attire is this army of the Lord of Hosts!"[8]

As a *famous* monk, though, Bernard was something of an anomaly, for the monk should live in holy leisure, removed from the hustle and bustle of ordinary society. He himself realized the contradiction in his own "monstrous" life; he called himself a "chimaera, neither cleric nor layman," who had kept the habit of a monk but abandoned the life.[9] Other fervent men avoided this dilemma by becoming canons regular (priests living under a *regula* or rule). They lived together in poverty, chastity, and obedience, but not in isolation. They saw around them a fluid society of growing towns, of new peasant settlements, of travelling pilgrims, a society moving away from the isolation of the monasteries. They went where the people were,

9

to preach, to administer sacraments, to found schools, to build hospices. Bernard was the last famous monk. After him, and before the mendicant friars of the thirteenth century, the stage was occupied by canons regular, of Premontré, of St. Victor, and of dozens of other houses.

That day at the abbey of Morigni, the other famous man was Abelard, already at odds with Bernard. Bernard said of him, "We have in France one Peter Abelard, a monk without a rule, a prelate without responsibility, an abbot without discipline, who argues with boys and consorts with women."[10] There was some truth in each of these charges, but they could not diminish Abelard's skill or his fame. His early promise of becoming the most renowned logician and teacher in Christendom had been fulfilled. His affair with Heloise and subsequent castration had nearly destroyed him, but students flocked to him, even when he retreated into the wilderness.

Indeed, they flocked to dozens of masters in France, for the appetite for learning was insatiable in the twelfth century, and France came to be the favorite feeding place of men like "Peter the Eater" (Petrus Comestor), who devoured books. As the century opened, most of the famous schools of Europe were in France: the Norman abbey of Bec, the cathedral schools of Rheims, Laon, Orléans, and Chartres. They were rivalled only by the abbey school of Monte Cassino, the law school in Bologna, and the medical school in Salerno. As the century closed, the various schools of Paris—Notre Dame, Ste. Geneviève, St.

Victor—were on the verge of becoming one, the university of Paris, the mistress of studies for all of Europe. The scholars were by no means entirely "French"; Peter Lombard came from northern Italy, Hugh of St. Victor from Saxony, Richard of St. Victor from Scotland, John of Salisbury from England. But for some reason, France seemed to be the favorite home for scholars.

Like other parts of Europe in the twelfth century, France was developing, in embryonic form, the interrelated complexities of modern society. As the population became more dense, the social organizations necessarily became more complicated. More thought was needed to keep these organizations functioning smoothly, and in the towns and princely courts, including the courts of ecclesiastical princes, the first bureaucracies began to develop. These new governments suppressed some of the violence which had characterized an earlier age (when violence was the only means to defend one's rights) and provided courts as an alternative. The growing commerce between regions and between town and country required that additional money be put in circulation, that institutions such as markets, fairs, and banking be developed to facilitate exchange. It also provided the wealth to support the urban and princely bureaucracies which supervised and protected the exchange. On every level, educated men were needed, men who could keep records and accounts, formulate rules and regulations, gather testimony and give judgments. Young men flocked to the schools in the hope of rising to positions of power and affluence in these budding bureaucracies, positions like those of Suger, abbot of St. Denis and regent of "France" under Louis VII, or of Walter of Coutances, archbishop of Rouen and chief justiciar of England under Richard the Lion-Hearted. The sons of townsmen who sought their fortunes in business aspired to positions less exalted but almost as comfortable. They too usually began their careers with letters and numbers. As happens today, some of these men succeeded in the world of affairs, some turned to learning and teaching, some simply lived lives of unfulfilled promise and disappointed hopes. But their combined efforts created a sizeable group of educated men who, together with the literate men and women of aristocratic courts, provided both the seed-bed and the audience for the many writers who took love as their subject.

Modern scholarship rightly stresses the accomplishments of twelfth-century France. The prosperous towns, the great stone churches, the overflowing schools, and the powerful, sophisticated courts were solidly based in a flourishing and expanding economy—indeed a likely setting for a fruitful interest in love. But the chronicles of the period prevent us from rashly calling it a century of love. It was also one of poverty and suffering, of ignorance and cruelty.

The modern city-dweller has almost forgotten his dependence on agricultural cycles. Rapid transportation and modern methods of preserving foods have made our diets relatively unchanging all year round. Consequently, we give most of our attention to irregular business cycles, cycles which affect our scale of living much more than the cycle of seasons which governs agriculture. But in the twelfth century, the success of a year's crop meant feast or famine to the people of the region. In 1109, food prices in the region of Sens were twice that of the previous year because storms of wind and hail had ruined fields, orchards, and vineyards.[11] For almost a decade before the second crusade (1147), food shortages in a province near the monastery of Trois-Fontaines forced nobles to sell all they had to survive and sent the lowly by the hundreds to beg bread from the monks.[12] Regional famines were a commonplace of twelfth-century France.

Warfare was perhaps a greater threat than the weather. Nothing was more common than for quarrelling nobles to destroy their enemies' economic resources, that is, to burn crops and buildings, together with any peasants and animals who happened to get in the way. The farmers always suffered. For the nobles, warfare was a rather enjoyable sport which relieved the tedium of peace, but, writes a chronicler, "quiet safety brought joy to the hearts of farmers."[13]

Even when the weather was good and the nobles were formally at peace, life was far from secure. Large bands of brigands, who respected nothing, terrorized the countryside like wolf-packs. In 1166, a group of them beset Cluny itself. When the monks led out a procession of burghers, trusting only in the relics they carried and the holy vestments they wore, the brigands fell upon them. They stripped the monks and killed the burghers. Louis VII caught some of them and hung them on gibbets to die, but no prince could hope to rid the land of all of them.[14] In 1183, an army of desperate people from all classes succeeded in cornering and massacring a force of brigands numbered at 10,000; but the 500 women who were found at the nearby camp probably had little trouble finding new camps to follow.[15]

The following pages are intended to reveal some of the tenderness, wisdom, and beauty of twelfth-century France; but the reader should remember that there was a darker side. Jews were massacred; captured peasants had their eyes put out; human and bestial enemies were cursed in elaborate "religious" rituals; fire, plague, and famine were never far away. This medieval paradox, in which beauty and ugliness live together with familial intimacy, no doubt disturbs us, but we cannot really complain until we resolve the paradox of our own cities, the modern homes of compassion and brutality, of erudition and illiteracy, and of luxury and poverty.

Finally, the reader should also remember that the twelfth century is only part of the so-called "middle ages." Authors frequently use the adjective *medieval* to apply to the fifth and fifteenth centuries alike, as though the millennium between had changed nothing. Anthologies of "medieval" writings place descriptions of ninth-century peasants next to those of fifteenth-century townsmen, as though nothing separated them but a town-wall and a stretch of forest. When the twelfth century began, St. Augustine had been dead for nearly 700 years, Charlemagne for nearly 300.

When it ended, Dante's *Divine Comedy* was still a century in the future, Chaucer's *Canterbury Tales* another century after that. This, then, is not a book about the "middle ages," that drab shroud commonly thrown over the varied colors of a thousand years. It is about the twelfth century only, a time when the rest of Europe looked to France for instruction on love. This small volume can lead the reader through the monasteries, the aristocratic courts, and the towns of France; but it can neither exhaust the varieties of love in twelfth-century France nor present them as a wholly consistent expression of a harmonious society. There was too much change, too much variety, too much conflict. Much less could it include Gregory the Great, Bede, Francis of Assisi, Thomas Aquinas, Dante, Petrarch, Wyclif, Chaucer, Thomas à Kempis, and all those other "medieval" students of love who lived outside twelfth-century France.

CHAPTER TWO

Love in the Legacy
from the Past

THE CULTURAL legacy inherited by the twelfth century was largely unwritten. Illiterate French knights treasured stories of their Frankish ancestors who rode with Charlemagne in campaigns against the Moslems, campaigns whose grandeur increased with each telling. From the misty highlands of Wales and from Ireland, where the Celts had taken refuge first from the Romans, then from the Angles and Saxons, and finally from the Normans, other tales of the fabled past filtered into France: tales of a great Celtic warrior named Arthur who had long, long ago withstood the Saxon invaders of Britain; tales of the ill-starred lovers Tristan and Iseult; tales of dragons, of magic springs, of bridges made of sharp swords, and of magic potions of every variety. The old German and Celtic stories were told and retold through the centuries, changing their shapes like the flames flickering before the listeners' eyes: crude and formless at one telling, artful at another, sometimes a short vignette, other times, as the late-autumn evenings grew longer, becoming long, complex, with countless digressions. They were the legacy of everyone, even of the illiterate. But an even more awesome treasure awaited the man of learning.

Learning to read is a heady experience. The modern child at first feels wonder as meaning leaps out from the markings that surround him. But the written word is cheap in our world, and he soon exhausts the wonder by reading trifles. In medieval Europe, the written word was rare. There was no daily accumulation of newspapers and circulars, no billboards in the fields and forests. The twelfth-century student who wanted to read had to go to the monastic and cathedral libraries and there turn the carefully cured and bound pieces of sheepskin on which the wisdom of antiquity had been preserved. Awe for the written word was there surely magnified, for those manuscripts were the fruits of countless hours of labor by the patient monks who copied and recopied them through the centuries.

The contents of the manuscripts confirmed the reader's respect, for nearly all of these works had been written by the pagan and Christian authors of Greco-Roman antiquity. They were the products of a civilization far more cultivated than that of the twelfth-century reader. Small wonder, then, that the written word was revered—the inspired words of the Bible and of the great Christian saints, but hardly less, the words of pagan writers, whose wisdom and art seemed almost to compensate for their lack of faith. To understand twelfth-century thinkers, then, we must begin where they began, with the contents of the libraries.

The presence of pagan authors in monastic libraries needs explanation. Christians of the later Roman Empire, from about 300 to 600, might have rejected the legacy of pagan antiquity; instead, they had decided that the intellectual products of the pagan past should be preserved and integrated into a Christian framework. Young Christians were educated in the "liberal arts," studying the literature, rhetoric, philosophy, mathematics, and science of the Greco-Roman tradition. Christian libraries throughout the middle ages preserved at least some of the texts necessary for that educational tradition, and the intellectual heritage of pagan antiquity thereby survived.

The pagan author of first importance was Plato. From Plato, Christians learned to describe man's love of God. He was not widely read in the twelfth century, for only one of his works, the *Timaeus,* was available in Latin (and hardly anyone read Greek), but Platonisms and Neoplatonisms were everywhere. Plato's principal ideas were that the immaterial soul was imprisoned in the body and that it yearned to be joined to the Absolute Good or Beautiful. All of life was a struggle of the soul to detach itself from the material in order to pursue the spiritual. These ideas were so congenial to Christian thought that nearly all Christian thinkers before the thirteenth century could be considered Platonists. Medieval readers found these ideas in both the Christian and the pagan authors of Rome. For example, a fifth-century pagan named Macrobius, read throughout the middle ages, spoke of "that discipline which directs philosophers to seek that sort of death in which, while still living, they despise the body as an extraneous burden."[1] Through St. Augustine, Macrobius, Boethius, and others, the Platonic tradition was preserved, many-formed and ever-present, and it provided a fundamental idea about love: the Christian's love for God was like that yearning of the soul for the Good which Plato called *eros*.

Aside from Plato, the most influential pagans were the Latin writers of Roman civilization, writers whose works could be read directly. In the works of Virgil, Ovid, Horace, and Cicero, the medieval reader encountered many themes of human love. The most important can be listed like this: love as overriding, passionate desire; love as mere sexual pleasure; love as a rational, non-erotic relationship between high-minded men. Significantly missing, we might add, was a theme which stressed marriage as an expression of love. In general, the Romans had a higher regard for marriage than did the Greeks before them, but the literati left discussions of marriage to the lawyers. Marriage formed political and economic ties between Roman families and provided offspring, but it was not often based on love and was not a favorite subject for literature. Marriage, which was rational and orderly, was a lawyer's business; the poets were interested in love.

The lover's passionate desire to possess the beloved

was probably encountered most frequently in the story of Aeneas and Dido in Virgil's *Aeneid.* Virgil told of how the gods had sent the Trojan hero Aeneas to found Rome after the destruction of Troy. His fleet was blown ashore near Carthage, whose Queen Dido found in Aeneas not only a defender against the importunate king of Numidia but a lover as well. She hoped he would stay with her as king of Carthage, a hope which Aeneas did little to dispel. But the gods called Aeneas back to his duty, and as he sailed away from Carthage, Dido mounted her funeral pyre and killed herself with her lover's sword.

The same kind of passionate love—bittersweet, beautiful, dangerous—recurs often in Ovid's *Metamorphoses,* a treasury of pagan mythology read throughout the middle ages. In one story, for example, Byblis is overcome by an unnatural love for her brother and flees into the wilderness until she falls exhausted. The naiads change her into a spring so that her tears will never stop flowing (9. 660–65). In another well-known story, Orpheus wins his dead bride, Eurydice, back from the underworld, with the provision that he lead her out without once looking back to see that she is following. At the last moment, "fearfully, hungry for the sight of her, he turned back his loving eyes—and instantly, she was lost." She made no complaint, for what complaint was there except that she was loved (10.57–61)?

Love involved taking delight in the beloved as well as feeling desire, but the Romans found, as have many moderns, that the force of love was more apparent in desire than in delight. The *joy* of the lover might be confounded with the joy of the hedonist, but *desire* separated the two. The hedonist did not allow himself the anguish of desiring what he might not have; the lover jeopardized everything for the sake of love. Dido lost her life for love; for love, Orpheus lost Eurydice, who was even more precious to him than life. For the most impressive characteristic of passionate love was this—that it seemed to override every other faculty and ideal of man. It was at times even more powerful than the desire for life itself.

Another theme in Roman literature was love as simple erotic pleasure. The main source for twelfth-century readers was Ovid's *Art of Love.* It is a handbook of seduction which describes in satirical, light-hearted tones how one goes about finding, winning, and keeping a mistress—or at least keeping her until one tires of her. Ovid advises his reader to frequent the theater, a place fatal to chastity. Having selected the lady, one bribes her maid and then lavishes time, promises, and flattery on the lady. Lavish everything but money. Since even the most chaste woman delights in her own beauty and believes false promises, the skillful seducer will have his way. After that, he need only avoid the lady's husband and try not to notice her other love affairs, and he is assured of keeping his mistress.

Satires of sexual mores will always be popular. They allow the reader to dabble vicariously in erotic misbehavior and at the same time to cluck his disapproval. And when the satire is the work of a poet of Ovid's caliber, its success is assured. The *Art of Love,* the *Metamorphoses,* and the other works of Ovid made him

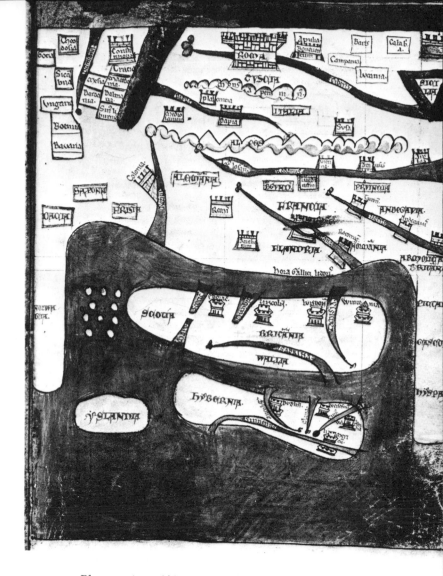

Plate 1. A twelfth-century conception of France, seen from the north. England is in the center, Flanders and France are above, and directly above them is Italy. Constantinople is in the upper left-hand corner, Spain is in the lower right-hand corner. Source: Dublin, National Library of Ireland, Ms. 100.

the most popular poet of pagan antiquity in the twelfth and thirteenth centuries, an era called by some scholars the "Ovidian Age." His works were sometimes given strange allegorical and mystical interpretations, so that the poet of Roman licentiousness became an unconscious spokesman of Christian morality, but he was also undoubtedly appreciated for what he was. In any case, he was quoted in the twelfth century by popes and poets, by saints and scholars.

Pagan antiquity provided a notion of love of quite a different sort, called *philia* in Greek, *amicitia* in Latin, and commonly translated as *friendship* in English. The subject was first treated extensively by Aristotle in the *Nicomachean Ethics* (books 8 and 9), but that work was not known in Western Europe until the thirteenth century. Aristotle's ideas made their way into the twelfth century via Cicero's dialogue *On Friendship*, a favorite of medieval readers.

Speaking through Laelius, the principal character of the dialogue, Cicero makes clear that friends show none of the blind irrationality of passionate lovers and none of the selfish deceit of calculating seducers. Friendship is based on the mutual recognition of virtue between two friends and it seeks no reward other than the love itself. Friendship is "harmony in all things, human and divine, together with good-will and affection" (6.20); and its effect is to "make one soul out of more than one" (25.92). It is both rare and precious. It can exist only among men of virtue and of similar character and tastes, no common combination, to be sure. But since friendship is excelled only by virtue itself, "we should always be searching for those whom we shall love and those who will love us in return" (27.104).

Throughout, Cicero never mentions women. Aristotle had allowed that there might be friendship between man and wife (*Nic. Ethics* 8.12), but it was necessarily an inferior friendship since women were by nature inferior to men. Cicero does not even mention the possibility, proposing instead an ideal of masculine virtue untainted by eroticism. Small wonder, then, that his ideas on friendship were to be extremely congenial to a Christian intelligentsia of celibate men.

Finally, the twelfth-century scholar who looked hard enough could find in his pagan authors another, much more comprehensive idea of love. Some of the ancients treated love as involving much more than the relationship between human beings. They saw it as a great cosmic force which explained the operation of the universe. Some stressed the generative power of love as the life-force of the universe. The prehistoric association of sexual energies with the sources of life, manifested in mother goddesses and fertility rites, lingered long after the goddesses and rites had been formally abandoned. Venus appeared as "the mother of all generations" in more than one of the pagan authors read in twelfth-century France.

A second cosmic interpretation of love saw it as the source of concord or harmony among the elements of the universe. One of the "best-sellers" of the twelfth century was *The Consolations of Philosophy,* written by

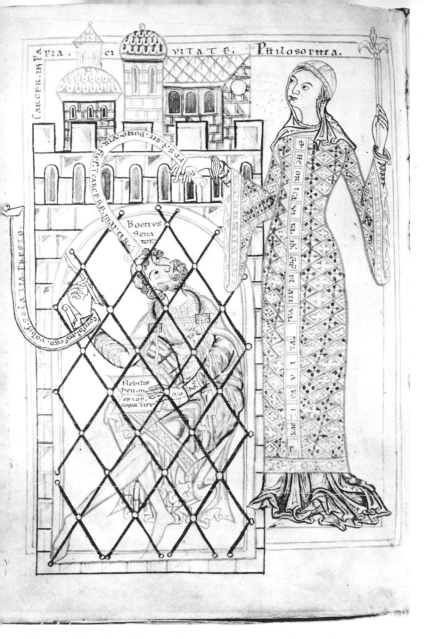

Plate 2. This detail from a German manuscript of around 1200 shows Philosophy visiting Boethius in prison. The inscriptions say that she offers him hope and he takes consolation from her visit. Source: Munich, Bayerische Staatsbibliothek, Cod. lat. 2599, fol. 106v.

Boethius, a Christian Roman of the late fifth century.
There could be read the following (Book II, poem 8):

> Love binds all things:
> The faithful earth adheres
> To its accepted changes;
> Unchanging laws hold in
> What warring seeds there are;
> Phoebus brings, in chariot
> Gold, the rosy day;
> Phoebe rules the nights
> Brought forth by Hesperus;
> The greedy sea restrains
> Its waves within its bounds
> Lest they infringe the broad
> Boundaries of shifting earth.
> Love rules the land and sea
> And dominates the heavens.
> If love let loose the reins,
> What moves now in love
> Would clash in sudden war;
> All would contend to smash
> The lovely motions of
> The order which they now,
> In love and trust, uphold.
> This love unites all peoples
> Under the holy law,
> Binds the sacred rite
> Of marriage in chaste loves,
> Lays down the laws of friendly
> Confidence for comrades.
> Oh man! What happiness
> If love which rules the heavens
> Ruled as well your souls!

The pagan tradition, then, provided its successor with several main themes of love. It was a spiritual longing for the Good which could not be satisfied in the material world; it was a passionate and erotic desire to possess the beloved; it was simple erotic pleasure, which should not be taken too seriously, lest it cease to be pleasurable; it was a reciprocal bond of good will and affection, possible between men of high character; on a cosmic scale, it was a mysterious force or power which generated all life in the universe and maintained harmony among its disparate parts.

All of these ideas were found in twelfth-century libraries; but the medieval reader found that Roman civilization had bequeathed to him Christian authors as well as pagan. By the end of the fourth century, the Roman Empire had become officially Christian. Some of the best minds of the day brought their talents, not to the faltering Empire, but to the rising Christian Church. St. Ambrose, a Roman statesman from a noble family in Gaul, became bishop of Milan. St. Jerome, born of wealthy parents in Illyria, received a superb Roman literary education and then used his skills to translate the Bible into Latin. And St. Augustine, born in Roman North Africa, abandoned a career as a distinguished teacher of classical rhetoric to become the bishop of his home town, Hippo. The works of these and other Christian Romans abounded in medieval libraries, and they passed on to the middle ages both the new Christian ideas of love and Christian variations on the pagan ideas already familiar.

27

The main well of Christian thought was the Judeo-Christian Bible, and Jerome assured that it would be available to the medieval centuries by translating it from Hebrew and Greek into Latin. His "Vulgate" translation was the most revered source possessed by twelfth-century readers. They puzzled over it, they quarrelled about it, but they never doubted that it was the word of God.

The Bible gave love a primacy in human affairs unmatched in any other philosophical or religious tradition. The God of the Old Testament was not only a just and faithful God, but a loving God. "I have loved you with an everlasting love," he told his people (Jer. 31:3), and he expected love in return: "You shall love the Lord your God with all your heart, and with all your soul, and with all your might" (Deut. 6:5). But whereas love is only one of many themes of the Old Testament, the New Testament is a rich collage of texts on love, bound together by the single theme that "God so loved the world that he gave his only Son" (John 3:16), and that man's response should be one of unmeasured love: "You shall love the Lord your God with all your heart, and with all your soul, and with all your mind. This is the great and first commandment. And a second is like it, You shall love your neighbor as yourself. On these two commandments depend all the law and the prophets" (Matt. 22:37–40). The primacy of love is inescapable:

> If I speak in the tongues of men and of angels, but have not love, I am a noisy gong or a clanging cymbal. And if I have prophetic powers and understand all

mysteries and all knowledge, and if I have all faith, so as to remove mountains, but have not love, I am nothing. If I give away all I have, and if I deliver my body to be burned, but have not love, I gain nothing. ... So faith, hope, love abide, these three; but the greatest of these is love (I Cor. 13:1–3,13).

And John says succinctly, "God is love" (I John 4:8).

The twelfth-century reader saw his Bible first through the eyes of its translator, Jerome, but also through the eyes of its great interpreters, the other "Latin Fathers of the Church": Ambrose, Gregory, and, most of all, Augustine. Christian love was easily seen to be a complicated matter, and Augustine was for medieval readers a favorite guide through its complications.

First of all, there was God's love for man, a subject on which the pagans had little to say. In the epistles of St. Paul and in the writings of St. Augustine, God's love is all giving. The act of creation was an expression of God's love which was totally one-sided; God's love for man preexisted man himself. After the Fall, when man was in need of redemption, God gave his son to effect man's salvation. Again, God acted freely to demonstrate a love which was in no way earned or deserved. And finally, there was the "gift of the Spirit" (a gift Augustine tended to identify with the Holy Spirit himself), which God sent to dwell in the hearts of the elect. Throughout, God's love for man is gift-love.

But if love is giving, how could man love God, for what did man have which God lacked? To answer this question, Augustine drew on his own experience and the Neoplatonic theories of a third-century Roman named Plotinus. Augustine had wandered from creed to creed seeking that intangible goal called happiness. He returned to Christianity believing he would find it through Christ, who was the way, the truth, and the life. He recorded these adventures in his unprecedented autobiography, *The Confessions,* the first page of which bears its theme: "Our hearts are restless until they rest in Thee." Man's love for God was not one of giving; it was rather that longing for the Good described by Plato and Plotinus, and its goal was union with the Good, now recognized by Augustine as the personal God revealed in Jesus. Man's love for God was the desire for and the delight in the Good.

The Christian who would love God, who would obtain the immaterial Good, must detach himself from material distractions lest he be forced to confess like Augustine, "While turned from thee, the One Good, I lost myself among a multiplicity of things."[2] Plotinus had expected the philosopher to lead a life of asceticism to facilitate the soul's movement up the "chain of being." Augustine expected the same discipline of the Christian, and offered as a reward the final beatitude after death and even, perhaps, some foreshadowing of that beatitude in this life, in the mystical experience of God. Paul had written with reserve of his own mystical experience:

> I know a man in Christ who fourteen years ago was caught up to the third heaven—whether in the body or out of the body I do not know, God knows. And I

know that this man was caught up into Paradise—
whether in the body or out of the body I do not know,
God knows—and he heard things that cannot be
told, which man may not utter (II Cor. 12:2-4).

This mystical communion was called *contemplation*
throughout the middle ages. It was heaven anticipated
on earth.

When Augustine turned to the second great commandment, the love of neighbor, he was somewhat
puzzled. His own experience was that human love was
dangerous, for one should love (desire and delight in)
nothing but God. Friendship could be a source of sin,
"while through an immoderate inclination toward
these goods of the lowest order, the better and higher
are forsaken. . . . "[3] At first, he said that only God is to
be loved for himself; other things are only to be used so
that they bring one closer to God. Then, faced with the
unavoidable requirement that he love and not just
"use" his neighbor, he developed the idea that crea-
tures should be loved in proportion to their position in
the hierarchy of existence. There was an order of love,
ordo amoris; created goodness and beauty helped lift
one's mind to their creator. But, however affectionate
Augustine may have been in his own life, his theories
did not readily incorporate love between humans in
this world. One's attention belonged to God, and one
was diverted from that goal only because the gospels
required man to tend to the physical and spiritual
needs of one's neighbor—a "giving" love akin to God's
love for man.

Essentially the same view of Christian love is found

in the works of Gregory the Great (d. 604), an author revered in the twelfth century only slightly less than Augustine. Gregory was a monk; and his writings helped define the monastic ideal, the highest Christian ideal from Gregory's day until the thirteenth century. Like Augustine, Gregory saw love as the soul's desire for and delight in God. Of contemplation, Gregory said, "When the mind tastes that inward sweetness, it is on fire with love."[4] The soul was purified and weaned away from worldly attachments by a life of asceticism and by the tribulations and temptations sent or allowed by God. The process begun on earth was completed only in heaven.

To Gregory, as to Augustine, the requirement to love one's neighbor meant to minister to his needs, and of course his spiritual needs came first. It was Gregory who took the paradoxical step of using monks, men dedicated to a life of withdrawal from the world, as missionaries to convert the world. He sent Augustine of Canterbury to England, and from the new monasteries founded there Benedictine monks soon came back to the continent to convert the heathen Germans. During the entire middle ages, love of neighbor meant first of all his conversion to the Christian life, for conversion meant salvation, and no greater gift could be given.

The love between God and man and between man and his neighbor clearly had nothing to do with erotic love. That was another matter, and it was a problem. The Christian legacy on sexual love was ambiguous. The twelfth-century reader might easily conclude from his sources that sexual love, marriage, women, and even matter itself were evil, but he might also discover, if he read more carefully, that such conclusions would be heretical.

The disapproval of sexual love had several sources. The early Christians were no doubt repelled by the licentiousness of much of Roman society. In any case, there was a strong tendency to asceticism founded in Stoicism and Neoplatonism and confirmed by the Bible. In Neoplatonism, especially, the soul reached its goal by moving "upward," away from the body and its concerns. The New Testament seemed to recommend complete sexual abstinence. Jesus and his mother were believed to be virgins, and Jesus spoke somewhat obscurely of those "who have made themselves eunuchs for the sake of the kingdom of heaven" (Matt. 19:12). Paul is quite explicit, and his first epistle to the Corinthians is so basic for medieval thought that it should be quoted at length:

It is well for a man not to touch a woman. But because of fornication, each man should have his own wife and each woman her own husband. The husband should give to his wife what is owed, and likewise the wife to her husband. For the wife does not rule over her own body, but the husband does; likewise the husband does not rule over his own body, but the wife does. Do not refuse one another except perhaps by agreement for a season that you may devote yourselves to prayer; but then come together again, lest Satan tempt you through lack of self-control. I say this by way of concession, not of

33

command. I wish that all were as I myself am. But each has his own special gift from God, one of one kind and one of another.

To the unmarried and the widows I say that it is well for them to remain single as I do. But if they cannot excercise self-control, they should marry. For it is better to marry than to burn.

To the married I give charge, not I but the Lord, that the wife should not separate from her husband (but if she does, let her remain single or else be reconciled to her husband)—and that the husband should not divorce his wife. . . .

I want you to be free from anxieties. The unmarried man is anxious about the affairs of the Lord, how to please the Lord; but the married man is anxious about worldly affairs, how to please his wife, and his interests are divided. And the unmarried woman or girl is anxious about the affairs of the Lord, how to be holy in body and spirit; but the married woman is anxious about worldly affairs, how to please her husband. I say this for your own benefit, not to lay any restraint upon you, but to promote good order and to secure your undivided devotion to the Lord (I Cor. 7:1–11, 32–35.)

The meaning of these passages has been much debated, especially since the Protestant Reformation, but throughout the medieval centuries they were nearly always taken to be a divine call to the celibate life. And later writers did not always preserve Paul's moderate tone. The love of woman was the earthly attachment Augustine found most difficult to cast off, and he described his deliverance like this, "Now was my soul free from the biting cares of canvassing and getting, and weltering in filth, and scratching off the itch of lust."[5] Generations of monks read these words, just as they read of the temptations of St. Anthony, an Egyptian monk of the third and fourth centuries whom the devil tried to entrap by taking the form of a beautiful woman. The celibate, who knew that the flesh lusted against the spirit, was often tempted to hate the body that he strove to master, to contemn the sexual appetites that disturbed his peace, and to suspect woman, the universal temptress, who first betrayed Adam and the human race and who continued to be a trap for the unwary Christian. In the New Testament, Paul had required women to cover their heads in church (I Cor. 11:5–15). St. Ambrose, the friend and counsellor of Augustine, explained:

> Since she is not the image of God a woman ought, therefore, to veil her head, to show herself subject. And since falsehood began through her, she ought to have this sign, that her head be not free, but covered with a veil out of reverence for the bishop. . . . Because of the beginning of crime, she ought to appear subject before a bishop, since he is the vicar of the Lord, just as she would before a judge.[6]

The inheritance from antiquity, then, cast a cloud of suspicion over sexual love, over marriage, over women, and even over the body itself.

On the other hand, one could not condemn matter and the body without being guilty of the Manichaean heresy, a heresy Augustine was at pains to repudiate. The Bible itself left little doubt that God had created

35

all matter, including the bodies of men (and of women), and that he had charged mankind to replenish the earth. Moreover, there was the metaphor of Paul that compared the relationship between husband and wife with that between Christ and the Church: "Husbands, love your wives, as Christ loved the church and gave himself up for her" (Ephes. 5:25). This metaphor implied a higher status for married love than was usually admitted in Christian circles. And then there was, in the Old Testament, the *Song of Songs,* whose sensuality was in strange and striking contrast with the asceticism of early Christianity. Compare the remarks of Augustine and Ambrose, quoted above, with this passage from the *Song of Songs,* (also called the *Canticle of Canticles* or the *Song of Solomon*):

> How fair and pleasant you are,
>   O loved one, delectable maiden!
> You are stately as a palm tree,
>   and your breasts are like its clusters.
> I say I will climb the palm tree
>   and lay hold of its fruit.
> Oh, may your breasts be like
>   clusters of the vine,
>   and the scent of your breath like apples,
> And your kisses like the best wine
>   that goes down smoothly,
>   gliding over lips and teeth (7:6–9).

The *Song of Songs* was a favorite of twelfth-century monks, perhaps because it was the only frankly erotic piece that they could read without hesitation—it was

Plate 3. Christ embracing the Church, an illustration from a twelfth-century copy of a commentary on the Song of Songs *by the eighth-century English monk Bede.* Source: *King's College, Cambridge, Ms. 19, fol. 21v. Photo courtesy Edward Leigh, Cambridge.*

the Bible, after all—but even more because it was taken to be an allegorical expression of Christ's love for his bride the Church, or for the individual soul. In the twelfth century, dozens of commentaries were written on the *Song of Songs,* all of them based on allegorical interpretations. Whatever their meaning, passages like these, combined with the Church's official condemnation of Manichaeism, provided that the Christian inheritance on sexual love was not totally one-sided. It was ambiguous.

Friendship was another form of love discussed by the early Christians. Cicero's theories on friendship were well-known, but they were not readily adaptable to either love of God or love of neighbor. Cicero's friendship rested on likeness in virtue between friends, and Augustine could see no such thing between God and man. Moreover, it was as obvious to Christians as it had been to Cicero that most neighbors were sadly lacking in virtue and therefore did not qualify for friendship. Still, his remark that friendship made "one soul out of many" struck Christian writers. Augustine was very conscious that friendship, like the other good things of this world, was transitory and insecure, but it was sweet nevertheless, because "of the unity formed of many souls." When describing heaven, his words, echoing Cicero's, suggest that he saw friendship as an essential part of that heavenly peace, "in which self-love and self-will have no place, but a ministering love that rejoices in the common joy of all, of many hearts makes one, that is to say, secures a perfect concord."[7]

The other Christian writers would no doubt have agreed that perfect friendship would only be realized in heaven, but three of them in particular discussed friendship in this world and passed on to the middle ages Christian variations of Cicero's ideas. The three are Ambrose, Jerome, and Cassian, and the principal variation from Cicero found in all three was that "virtue" was no longer that of a Roman aristocrat but was now defined in Christian terms. Likeness in virtue was most likely to be found among Christian ascetics—humble men and women who embraced poverty and chastity. A second variation was that friendship was now a goal for all to pursue, since the necessary virtue was not the exclusive property of those endowed with virtuous natures. It was available to anyone who would accept the Gospel and be perfected by God's grace. It was no longer an aristocratic preserve. These changes were not always spelled out by the Christian authors, but they were clearly implicit in what they said about friendship.

Bishop Ambrose of Milan wrote *The Duties of Ministers,* a handbook for clergymen. While discussing honesty, he asks whether one may be dishonest for the sake of friendship. His answer is "no," of course, but in saying so he offers a few pages on friendship.[8] Himself an ecclesiastical statesman reared in the Roman tradition, he differed little from Cicero, except that he buttressed Cicero's ideas with Biblical quotations: "A faithful friend is an elixir of life, a gift of immortality" (Eccles. 6:16).

Ambrose does seem to go beyond Cicero somewhat in

39

stressing the intimacy and self-revelation of friendship. Open your heart to your friend, he advises; commit to your friend the secrets of your heart; the true friend reveals his soul just as Jesus revealed the mysteries of the Father. This special emphasis probably appears because his main subject is not friendship but honesty.

Jerome provided a similar Christian variation on Ciceronian friendship in his extensive correspondence with close personal friends. Although he defined virtue in Christian terms, he considered friends as rare as did Cicero, and as much to be treasured. To his "beloved Rufinus" he wrote, "I beg you not to let this friend be out of mind as I am out of sight, for a friend is long sought for, rarely found, and easily lost."[9] A striking novelty appears when Jerome includes women among his friends, beginning a Christian tradition of love as friendship among celibate men and women. He was the spiritual counsellor of a number of Roman women, and the affection that developed between some of the women and their advisor was warm enough to bring charges of impropriety. Jerome defended himself against scandalmongers, saying with irony, "Before I became acquainted with the household of the saintly Paula, all Rome was enthusiastic about me. . . . But when, recognizing the holiness of her life, I began to revere, respect, and venerate her, all my good qualities at once forsook me."[10] Jerome wrote a number of affectionate letters to Christian women. They were read throughout the middle ages and provided justification for the exchange of letters, mementos, and poems among nuns, clerics, and monks.

In the works of Cassian, the idea of friendship has passed further from the spirit of Cicero.[11] Cassian came from the Danubian provinces of the Empire, had lived in monastic communities in Bethlehem and Egypt, and had passed several years as a disciple of St. John Chrysostom in Constantinople. He went to Rome about 405, only a few years before Alaric's looting armies, and then to Marseilles, one of the Roman cities that did not fall into the hands of invading Vandals and Visigoths. There he founded his monastery of St. Victor the Martyr, and the spirit of Egyptian monasticism was introduced into the West.

The enduring influence of Cassian's works was due to another monk, St. Benedict, the founder of Monte Cassino. About 529, a century after the death of Cassian, Benedict wrote a rule for his monks, and the Rule of St. Benedict was to be the basic constitution for nearly every European monastery for centuries to come. The Rule has much to say about obedience and humility and remarkably little to say about love. Benedict seems to have learned from Cassian, who was his favorite author, the idea that obedience and humility produced virtue, and whenever there was virtue there was love. In any case, he admits the incompleteness of his Rule and urges his monks to read the Bible and the Fathers, including the *Conferences* of Cassian, the work containing the treatise on friendship. As a consequence, Cassian continued to be read wherever the Rule was observed.

In his treatise, Cassian reports the instructions of an ancient Egyptian monk named Joseph, steeped in the learning of Egypt and Greece, and Cassian speaks through Joseph just as Cicero had spoken through Laelius. Like Cicero, Cassian saw virtue as the source of friendship, but the Christian monk, writing for a monastic audience, necessarily meant something different. Unlike Cicero, and even unlike Ambrose and Jerome, Cassian was writing for men who could not choose their friends. Having decided to live out their days within monastic walls, they had to live in accord with a small circle of men whom nature and habit had shaped quite differently. Consequently, Cassian adjusted the proposition that friendship was based on likeness in virtue so that it meant: likeness in virtue will inevitably bring about friendship. If all the monks were alike in virtue, friendship, with its "oneness of will," would guarantee concord and peace to the monastery. Cassian warned, "Peace can never be preserved intact where there is diversity of wills."[12] Likeness in virtue for such a heterogeneous group would have struck Cicero as impossible, but for the Christian Cassian, virtue was the product not of nature but of God's grace and the persistent effort of the monk. If the monks wished to have the peace provided by friendship, let each one contemn the goods of this world, commonly the source of dissension; let him subordinate his own will to the discipline of the monastery, so that he be less fond of his own ways of doing things and more adaptable to the ways of his brothers; let him put love and peace before all else; let him never succumb to anger himself and let him do all he can to dispel the anger conceived against him by his brother; let him distrust his own judgment and place his trust in the older monks; and let him ever remember that he is each day migrating from this world to the next.

Friendship, as described by Cassian, is primarily peace and concord. There is little in his treatise to suggest the personal intimacy, the pleasure of a friend's company, found in Cicero and Ambrose. Cassian would, it is true, allow a monk to extend greater affection to one than to another (while still loving all), but only on the basis of "merit." Individual tastes, inclinations, and manners were, rather than the bases of friendship, obstacles to friendship, and were to be obliterated by uniform adherence to the rule.

In practice, Cassian may have shown greater warmth and affection than his theories suggest. But, like Augustine he found any concern for his fellow man a distraction from what was more important:

> Who can with tranquil mind gaze upon the glorious majesty of God while engaged in works of charity? Who can contemplate the immeasurable blessedness of heaven at that very moment when he is ministering alms to the poor, when he is welcoming visitors with gracious hospitality, when he is concerned with caring for the needs of his brethren?[13]

Most of the early Christians balance their praise for human love with this wariness of earthly attachments, perhaps unable to forget the evangelical warning, "He who loves father or mother more than me is not worthy of me" (Matt. 10:37–38).

The legacy from Christian Romans, then, contained some ideas on love which were similar to pagan ideas, and some which were quite different. The Christian love for God was similar to the pagan love for the Good. Christian suspicions of sexual love, even in marriage, were derived in part from pagan philosophies, and Christians condemning Roman licentiousness echoed their pagan countrymen. And the Christian spectrum included some acceptance of sexual love and a somewhat more generous acceptance of Ciceronian friendship.

On the other hand, Christianity introduced entirely new ideas into the pagan world. First of all, the Christian God was, apart from his goodness, radically different from the Good of Plato and Plotinus. He was a God of three persons, who loved one another without losing their divine unity. He was a personal and loving God who intervened in human life through his "grace." The central intervention was the Incarnation, God become man, an intervention which would enable man to reach his "supernatural" goal. There is none of this notion of a loving God in the pagans.

Secondly, the Christian *commandment* to love was something new. For the pagan, love was the spontaneous reaction of the noble soul when brought into the presence of something or someone good or beautiful, or else the equally spontaneous sexual desire for the sexually desirable. For the Christian, the spontaneous reactions of a fallen nature were not to be trusted. For him, the commandment to love meant that man was free to love or not to love, and it required man to exert himself rather than wait for spontaneous movements of love. Gregory the Great described the difficult stages through which the soul went in achieving love of God: "Whoever has already subdued the insolencies of the flesh in himself, has this task left him, to discipline his mind by the exercises of holy working; and whosoever opens his mind in holy works, has over and above to extend it to the secret pursuits of inward contemplation."[14]

None of this was possible without God's grace, and one can argue that early Christianity passed on a logical contradiction when it asserted on the one hand that God was the source of all love, that man's love was really God's love in him, and on the other hand that man was free to love or not to love. But the fact remains that medieval Christianity always assumed that it was man's responsibility to love and that love was the fruit of human effort as well as of divine intervention. The Christian recipe for love was human nature and divine grace; the proportions were not clearly described. In any case, man was free to love or not to love.

And finally, love among humans had at once a higher and a lower place in Christian thought than it did in pagan circles. Christians accepted the obligation to love all men, even their enemies and the most contemptible sinners, notions utterly foreign to the pagans. On the other hand, this kind of love was often an impersonal benevolence; and Christians did not give human friendship, with its mutual affection and companionship, the same value as the pagans did. As a reciprocal relationship between equals, friendship was somehow different from the love of God or the love of neighbor, the first obligations of the Christian.

The legacy in medieval libraries was, then, an ambiguous one. For the pagan authors, love was the spiritual desire for the Good, the passionate desire for the beloved, mere sexual pleasure, friendship, or possibly a cosmic force creating and ordering the universe. The Christian authors adopted and transformed the pagan ideas and added their own: love as an act of God, love as a moral requirement, which man should accept but could reject, and love as benevolence toward all men, generous but somewhat impersonal. These ideas survived in countless combinations into the twelfth century. The ancients did not make clear how these ideas were related to one another, nor did they achieve a thoroughgoing reconciliation or synthesis. That impossible task is part of the inheritance of Western civilization.

CHAPTER THREE

The Monasteries

THE MONK'S life was intended to be a life of love. Each day he went through the routine prescribed by the Rule of St. Benedict, a routine of sleeping and eating, praying, reading, and working. Each day he was called upon to consider the purpose of his life: to know and love God. The good monk lived in the personal presence of the God who made him, who knew him, who loved him, and who would one day judge him. The monastic life was acknowledged by all to be the best way for a man to respond to this presence. The monk read in the Old Testament of how the Hebrews anticipated the Promised Land and the Messiah, he thought of his own exile in this world of hardship and suffering, and he longed for the heavenly kingdom of the Father. He read of the kindness, patience, and love of Jesus, and he was moved to remorse for his own egotism and petty selfishness. He thought of how the life, death, and resurrection of Jesus made possible the opportunity of unending happiness in heaven, where there would be peace and joy and love. And the monk's heart filled with gratitude and with love for the compassionate Father who sent the Son, for the humble Son who was obedient even unto death, and for the loving Holy Spirit who continued to warm the hearts of all believers.

Only the monk's belief in the personal presence of a God who loved and wanted to be loved gave meaning to the monastic life. The monk William of St. Thierry wrote to a community of Carthusian monks: "This is your profession, to seek out the God of Jacob—not in the ordinary manner of men, but to seek the face of God as it was seen by Jacob, who said, 'I have seen God face to face, and my life has been saved.'" The Carthusian's cell, said William, was "a holy land and a holy place, where the Lord and his servant often talk together, like a man and his friend."[1] The schoolmen in the towns looked for God too, but they posed problems, they speculated and debated, they created elaborate theories about God and his universe. The monks were suspicious of all this. They cultivated the awareness of God's presence. Their attitude was not speculation, but admiration; their goal was not the formulation of a theology, but the experience of loving.

Of course not all monks were lovers. Monasteries were peopled in many ways. Some monks were left there as small boys by their parents. The father with too many sons, or with one too scrawny to be a good

48

knight, could take the vows on his son's behalf and thus provide for his offspring and for his own immortal soul (for every man of the world could use the prayers of a monk in the family). Some men, young and old, fled to the monasteries in fear, haunted by visions of the world, the flesh, and the devil, and of the fiery torments of hell that awaited the reprobate. The powers of darkness were ever present in twelfth-century France, and few men were so rash as to neglect the danger. The monk's cowl was generally acknowledged to be the best defense against Satan's horrors.

For others, the monasteries were simply homes. The rigors of monastic life in even a lax house would repel the modern, but they surely seemed less harsh to twelfth-century people. The monastery was often an island of order and security in an insecure world. The fare was often meager, but it was dependable. Most monastic houses were well-enough endowed that they were the last communities to go hungry in hard times. When famine came, the hungry went to the monastery with the assurance that there, if anywhere, would be food and the disposition to share it. The monk's life was hard, deprived of many of the ordinary joys of life, but it was also sheltered from many of the ordinary disasters.

Many monks who had little taste for poverty, chastity, or obedience led lives of open scandal or private self-indulgence. When Abelard tried to reform his monastery in Brittany, his monks tried unsuccessfully to kill him. Other monks were murderers in fact as well as intent. Monastic regulations provided elabo-

49

rate precautions to keep women out of the monasteries, and we can only guess how far the regulations were remedy and how far precaution. Monasteries for nuns had similar problems. The nunnery of St. Eloi near Paris acquired such a scandalous reputation that in 1107 the nuns were driven out and replaced by monks.[2] Scholars occasionally wrote love letters to nuns and to girls being tutored in convents, and although the correspondence may be nothing more than that, it showed that the nuns were certainly thinking about things other than the love of God.[3]

The main hazards for most monks, though, were probably not extravagant sins, but gradual relaxations of their discipline. Even the fervor of the best monks often cooled when, like married couples, they discovered that love was easily forgotten amid the trials and tedium of everyday life. The traditional vice of monks has not been lust but gluttony. The line between continence and fornication is easily drawn, but one can slip from moderation into gluttony or drunkenness through sheer inadvertence.

And even good monks were inclined to be quarrelsome. The twelfth century was a bellicose age, and the love of combat was not restricted to knights. Scholars hurled themselves into verbal combat with ferocity and enthusiasm, wielding the charge of heresy as a lethal weapon. Monks found their battles mainly in the courts of law. They showed a love of litigation that kept them returning again and again to judicial fields of combat, arguing over revenues or property or disputed elections. A new subject for quarrels was born when Cistercians and Cluniacs began to view each other as competitors. Their celebrated spokesmen, Bernard of Clairvaux and Peter the Venerable, conducted a debate on a fairly high level, each defending his own form of monasticism. On a lower level, some bawdy Cluniacs claimed that Cistercians wore no pants beneath their habits, not out of love of poverty but out of love of lechery.

How then can we characterize the monasteries? There was major and minor vice in them. There were surely many monks who, like many moderns, accepted with satisfaction the reasonable and orderly rhythm of their lives without probing too deeply into its meaning. But in their liturgy, in their reading, in their sermons, and in their correspondence, the monks met again and again the goals and ideals of monastic life. It was to be a life of love. The theme was inescapable in the legacy from the past, and it was taken up and reaffirmed with literary grace and deep perception by twelfth-century monks.

The most striking characteristic of monastic writing about love is that it is intensely introspective. The monks were familiar with the legacy from antiquity—with the second-century Greek Father Origen, with Augustine and Gregory—but they enriched it with the lessons of their own hearts. Bernard once remarked, "We read today in the book of experience," and another Cistercian wrote, "I think, brothers, that you have read in the book of your experience, in your heart rather than in a manuscript."[4] Much more than works coming from the schoolmen, monastic writing demonstrated the involvement of the whole personality in the experience of loving. Love grew from fear and gratitude, it caused joy and sorrow, it poured forth in songs and tears. The monastic habit of analyzing the movements of the soul is a major source of the western tradition of introspection, a tradition which has given rise to modern psychiatry and to much of modern literature.

The monks' sensitivity to the workings of the soul enabled them to see that love was not a static thing. It grew and developed—or waned. Moreover, they saw that although love was a natural inclination, its direction and intensity could be at least partially controlled. Oneness with God, the goal of monastic life, was the fruit of a long process. It was understood only through thought and prayer, realized only through effort and grace.

Beyond the empirically introspective and dynamic character of love, the monks held other ideas with which many modern readers will be less sympathetic. For one thing, the monks systematically excluded sexuality as a legitimate area of human experience. They were sensitive analysts, but, sworn to celibacy, they could only view erotic stirrings as unmitigated vice, which they consciously suppressed and unconsciously sublimated. After the final resurrection, when the glorified bodies of men would be cleansed of this obstinacy, soul and body would be in harmony. In the meantime, the monk could make no concession to his sexual inclinations, which he called, simply, lust.

A second idea that may seem foreign even to some

modern Christians is the immediate relevance of the doctrine of the Trinity to the experience of loving. Twelfth-century monks were quite consciously engaged in psychological engineering, in deliberately fostering in themselves attitudes and emotions which were by no means spontaneous. But in doing so, they never doubted that the Holy Spirit was supporting their efforts. Their struggle would be in vain unless he acted to unite them to the Father and the Son in some mysterious way remotely analogous to the way in which he united the Father and the Son to each other. Even today the oneness experienced between two lovers remains something of a mystery. Medieval monks, as the Latin fathers had done before them, associated the mysterious loving union of separate persons with the doctrine of the Trinity. The Holy Spirit was both the agent and the expression of that union.

The writings of two monks, Bernard, abbot of Clairvaux, and his friend, William, abbot of St. Thierry, are of particular importance for the topic of love. Their works on love were much sought after, and by the end of the century manuscript copies had found their way into monastic libraries all over Europe.

Bernard was surely the most remarkable man of his day. It was Bernard who, in the 1130s, organized European leaders in support of Pope Innocent II against his rival for the papacy, Anacletus II. It was Bernard who mobilized European knights in the 1140s and sent them to the Holy Land in the futile Second Crusade. He was probably the supreme moral authority in Europe in those decades, and he did not hesitate to use that authority to chasten kings and cardinals, scholars and bishops. Bernard moved with the astonishing self-confidence of those who believe themselves to be the instruments of God or of history. Many of his campaigns now seem misguided: his enthusiasm for the crusade, his condemnation of townsmen who tried to expand their liberties by rebelling against barons or bishops, his attacks upon the intellectuals Abelard and Gilbert de la Porrée. He assumed that political and social problems rooted in the complexities of history, which he had not studied, were as readily solved as those rooted in the complexities of the individual soul, which he had. But his devotional works remain as an achievement independent of his public life.

Love is prominent in all of Bernard's writing. References to "Lady Charity" fill his correspondence; he wrote a long series of sermons, each based on a verse from the *Song of Songs,* and love is never neglected in his many other works. One small treatise, though, was devoted exclusively to love. Probably written in the 1120s, it was entitled *On Loving God.*[5]

Bernard's theme in this work is why and how God should be loved, and he begins by examining the human condition. Man clearly enjoys many good things that he did not himself create. He has, especially, spiritual gifts unique among animals. He has first his dignity, derived mainly from free will, the power of intelligent choice. Through this gift man is not only pre-eminent among animals, but is able to preside over them. Secondly, man has knowledge, whereby he recognizes his own unique dignity, but at the same time recognizes that he is not himself the source of that dignity. And finally, man has virtue, whereby he seeks out the Creator of his dignity and clings to him when he has found him. If a man lacks the knowledge of his dignity, he is like an animal. If he knows of his dignity, but claims it as his own work, he is diabolic, for he would make himself God. But the man who perceives himself as God-created is led, through sheer gratitude, to the love of God.

Bernard believed that introspection can reveal all this to the infidel as well as to the Christian, so that, if nothing else does so, gratitude should lead all men to the love of God. For the Christian, the gratitude should be all the greater, because he knows God's generosity in the death and resurrection of Christ, who earned eternal life for those who believe. Whereas the infidel has only his experience to draw upon, the Christian has his memories. The bride in the *Song of Songs* pleaded, "Sustain me with flowers, comfort me with apples, for I am sick with love" (2:5). Christ the Bridegroom responds to the soul and consoles her with the "apples of his suffering" and the "flowers of his resurrection." With these memories, the soul is comforted until she enters into the embrace of the heavenly bedchamber. Bernard says, then, that any man should love God in gratitude and without measure, but especially the man who knows Christ, who is the fullness of God's generosity.

Besides gratitude for what we have, there is desire for what we lack. Bernard considers it natural that in

Plate 4. Jesus being taken from the cross. Reflecting on the sacrifice of Christ, the conscientious monk tried to feel the grief, compassion, and gratitude evidently felt by this artist. Source: Ingeborg Psalter, Chantilly, Musée Condé, Ms. 1695, fol. 27r. Photo courtesy Giraudon.

this world man wants more than he has. The impious man goes from thing to thing, always disappointed because nothing ever completely satisfies. Such a man might even get to God if he could obtain all creation, so that nothing was left but the Creator, but in fact he spends his too brief life in a burdensome and fruitless circuit. The material things he seeks nourish the soul no more than wind nourishes the body.

Only God can satisfy the spirit. He is the beginning of human love and its end. The man who loves God is rewarded with the satisfaction of his desires. He should not love God for the reward (for then he would be loving the reward more than God), but the love will nevertheless be rewarded. "True love does not require a reward, but it merits it nevertheless" (col. 984). And the man who loves God has already begun to possess him, for "here is the wonder of it all, that no one can seek you unless he has first found you (col. 987). The love of God is its own reward, experienced in part on earth and in its fullness in heaven.

Bernard found man's reasons for loving God by searching the soul of man. Using the same procedure, he recounted the stages through which love develops. Love is a natural inclination, to be sure, but it must move along proper channels, guided and impelled by man himself and by the direct and indirect action of God. Man begins with simple, egocentric carnal love. He wants his body to be well fed and comfortable. This self-love is wholly natural and good, so long as it does not overflow the channels of necessity into the fields of sensuality. This love matures into a more compre-

57

hensive carnal love as man comes to realize the interdependence of men for their material needs. His carnal love becomes social, embracing an interdependent community.

But man's limitations force him to look beyond human society to a greater power, and thus he moves to the second stage of love. The most capable individual or the most providential community cannot always escape disaster. God does not allow man to overlook his own inadequacy. By visiting suffering upon man, God forces him to see human dependence upon divine will. In this way, man's love, still self-centered, expands to include God, just as it had expanded to include the human community. The love of God, rooted in man's need, is the second stage of love.

Only when man has reached this stage is he ready to profit from the lesson earlier outlined by Bernard. Now he comes to see God's generosity in providing him with physical necessities, and, indeed, with his spiritual gifts. Now he comes to see and appreciate the goodness of God and begins to love God for his own sake. "For we have tasted and have seen how sweet is the Lord" (col. 989). This is the third stage of love, when man has gone beyond carnal love, when he has gone beyond loving God because of man's dependence on him and has come to love God because of what God is.

The fourth stage is a great blessing rarely achieved in this life. When the soul is drunk with divine love and loses all consciousness of self, when it is almost absorbed into God, it becomes one spirit with him.

There is an utter oneness of will between the soul and God. The fortunate soul who does have this experience in this life is soon recalled by the mundane needs of his brothers. But one day love will be experienced in its fullness. As water mixed with wine seems to become wine, as iron in fire seems to take on the form and the color of the flame, as air transfused with light seems to be the light itself, so will the soul be one with God. "The substance will remain, but in another form, another glory, another power" (col. 991).

Bernard expects this final glory after the resurrection, for until then even the soul with God will not be contented until reunited with the body, that "good and faithful companion of the soul" (col. 993). The invitation of the *Song of Songs,* "Eat, friends, and drink; and become inebriated, dear ones" (5:1), is God's invitation to man. The soul eats in this life, drinks in the next, and finally, when reunited with the body, is inebriated with love and lost in God. Even then, love is not static, but is eternally restless, while being at rest: "Hence that satisfaction without satiety, hence that eternal and inexhaustible desire which feels no want; hence finally that sober inebriation steeped not in drink but in truth—not soaking with wine but burning with God" (col. 995).

As a final chapter, Bernard appended a letter about love that he had written some time before to a community of Carthusians. The ideas are essentially the same as in the earlier chapters, although he stresses somewhat more the pervasive importance of love and finds another way of presenting the idea that love progresses through stages. Love is more than a mere gift of God, for it is God himself. "God is love," wrote John (1 John 4:8). Love is the law by which God lives, for "what is it in the supreme and blessed Trinity which preserves that supreme and ineffable unity, unless it is love?" Love is the "divine substance" (col. 996). As for the four stages of love, they are presented again in this final chapter, but Bernard also speaks of the "laws" of the slave, of the hireling, and of the son. The slave praises God out of fear, the hireling out of desire for reward, and the son out of love, because God is good. Perhaps Bernard's most acute perception here is that the law of the son, which is the law of love, does not destroy the other laws. That is, fear and desire remain, even in him who loves God for himself. But the fear is now a "chaste" fear, not fear of punishment but fear of losing the beloved. The desire is now an "ordered" desire. The love of God is an overriding love which puts all things in their proper places, so that "the body and all the good things of the body are loved for the sake of the soul, the soul for the sake of God, but God for the sake of himself alone" (col. 998).

For Bernard, love is gratitude for needs and desires fulfilled, for gifts given freely out of love; love is the desire and yearning of the human heart which can only be satisfied by God; love is the joy of possession and of being possessed, of oneness with the divine Bridegroom. And love is all these things at once; the knowledge of God, the desire for God, and the enjoyment of God are all inseparable, from their primitive origins in the beginner to their culmination in the final state, the marriage of man with the Word, when the two become one in spirit.

Every word of Bernard's discussion would have been seconded by his friend William, abbot of the Benedictine abbey of St. Thierry near Rheims. Although a few years his senior, William idolized Bernard and was prevented from joining him at the Cistercian abbey of Clairvaux only by Bernard's insistence that he should remain at St. Thierry where he was needed.

William's temperament was quite different from that of his friend. He joined Bernard in trying to rein in Abelard, but he never showed Bernard's supreme self-confidence or his mastery of others. His education had taken him to Laon probably at the time when the young Abelard was first making a name for himself by humiliating his teacher Anselm. William was repelled by the violence of academic disputations and by the arrogance of competitive young scholars matching wits with one another, so he left them all for the peace and benevolence of the monastery. He became abbot of St. Thierry in 1119, four years after Bernard had become abbot at Clairvaux; in 1135 he moved to the Cistercian house at Signy. The harshness of Cistercian life, which broke Bernard's health but never fazed his spirit, was almost too much for the less resilient William, but he endured until his death in 1148. His last years were spent in working on a life of Bernard.

William was no mere echo of Bernard; he was a man of learning and he wrote on a wide variety of subjects. But formed by the same learned and ascetic tradition as Bernard, and awed by Bernard's greatness, William was not likely to differ from him radically about love. His ideas and his metaphors are not identical with Bernard's, but the kind of love he describes is clearly the same.

William did not bother to explain in detail why God should be loved. He wrote for a monastic audience that shared his basic assumption that the love of God was the purpose of human life. William agreed with Ovid that love was the art of arts and that one needed instruction in this art, but, unlike Ovid, William was interested in the love that lifted man's soul from terrestrial concerns to the pursuit of God. He discussed the nature of this pursuit in several works, but especially in *On the Contemplation of God* and *On the Nature and Dignity of Love,* both written at St. Thierry, and in a letter written to a Carthusian community a few years before his death at Signy.[6] This letter, long mistaken for a work of Bernard's, was famous for centuries as the "Golden Letter," but the other two works were also widely read in European monasteries. Taken together, the three works provide us with a good source for monastic love.

Like Bernard, William thought love was the natural impulse toward goodness placed within the soul by nature, or by God, the author of nature. But love was easily corrupted by the weakness of the flesh unless it was carefully cultivated. Love must be taught, but not in the manner of Ovid, nor even in the manner of the schoolmen, too often given over to pride and rivalry rather than to love. In his letter to the Carthusians,

William commended them for their way of life and added, "Leave the wise men of this age—blown up with the spirit of this world, claiming to taste lofty wisdom while licking the earth—leave them to descend wisely into hell."[7] No, the place to learn the art of love was the monastery, for it was the special school of love. "Here the study of love is cultivated, its disputations are held, and the solutions are reached not by syllogisms but by reason and by real truth and by experience."[8]

The necessary lessons were given in the monastery. The monastic life required discipline for the body, so that it became the faithful servant of the soul. It required reading about the life of Jesus so that corporeal man, "who doesn't know how to think about anything which is not corporeal, may have something which he can relate to himself."[9] It required prayer for divine assistance. Without the intervention of the Holy Spirit, there could be no love of God. "Man does not love God except through the Holy Spirit. The love of God, therefore, which is born in man by grace, is nursed by reading, fed by meditation, and strengthened and adorned by prayer."[10]

Like Bernard, William looked for ways to describe love as something which develops. Love grows through stages, just as the boy develops into the youth, the youth into the man, and the man into the old man. He called these stages *will,* which grows into love, *love (amor),* which grows into charity, and *charity (caritas),* which grows into wisdom. Again, he spoke of five kinds of love analogous to the five senses of the body: carnal love (love of family), social love (love of fellow Christians), natural love (love of all men, all sharing the same nature), spiritual love (love of enemies, a love that does not grow out of nature), and divine love (love of God).[11] Borrowing from Origen, he wrote elsewhere of the three stages of the religious life: beginning, progressing, and perfected.[12]

Whatever metaphor William chose, the development is basically the same. Moved by fear (and grace), the beginner determines to love God. He labors and sweats in the monastic exercises, subduing the flesh, reading, meditating, praying, but he acts blindly, without any direct perception of why he does so. Gradually, however, he begins to develop an awareness of God. The Holy Spirit leads forth a new man who perceives the goodness of God and is untroubled by the demands of the flesh or by secular ambition. As the "new man" grows in wisdom, he comes to delight in the taste and flavor of God, almost "to touch with the hand of experience" the goodness of God.[13]

Like Bernard, William is aware that although love grows and changes, the experience of loving has a unity which is betrayed by rational analytic divisions. "It must be said that although one who ascends passes through stages to the citadel of wisdom, nevertheless, the will would not move, nor love continue, nor would contemplation come forth in charity nor delight in wisdom, if wisdom did not, in every stage up to the last, seek out those seeking her. . . . As we have begun with taste, we continue with taste." One does not leave one stage and pass to another; rather the stages concur to work together.[14] "For to see the good things of the lord is to love them, and to love them is to have them. So let us strive as best we can so that we may see, and by seeing understand, and by understanding love, and by loving have."[15]

Metaphors, not always consistent with one another, are necessary too for describing the loving union between man and God which begins on earth and is perfected in heaven. Man is one in likeness with God because he was created in God's image. But by sin man has passed into the "region of dissimilarity" and is therefore in need of the saving regimen of Christ provided in the monastery. The Eucharist makes man one with the body of Christ and thus a true son of the Father.[16] The Holy Spirit pours himself into the soul so that man becomes one spirit with God. As man becomes more like God, his own introspection reveals God through his human image, so that "man begins to know himself perfectly, and, by progressing in the knowledge of self, begins to ascend to the knowledge of God."[17] That ineffable union which begins in this life and culminates in the next is a oneness of body, oneness of spirit, and oneness of similarity. "What God is by nature, man is by grace."[18]

Bernard and William are only two of many monks to describe the love of God.[19] In 1142, the English Cistercian Ailred of Rievaulx passed through France on his way to Rome and was instructed by Bernard to write a treatise on love. His *Mirror of Charity* describes man's progress to God as progress from one sabbath to another:

Plate 5. The Last Judgment. Just as the suffering Christ had risen in glory, the monk hoped to overcome death and suffering at the Last Judgment. Source: *Ingeborg Psalter, Chantilly, Musée Condé, Ms. 1695, fol. 33r. Photo courtesy Giraudon.*

In each Sabbath we find rest and peace and joy for the spirit, but the first belongs to a man's own quiet conscience, the second to a community of men living happily together, and the third consists in the contemplation of God. The first sabbath is rest from sin, the second is rest from cupidity and the third is rest from every sort of dissension. In the first one we taste and see how sweet the manhood of Jesus is. In the second we see how perfect and complete is His charity. In the third we see Him as He is in Himself, as God. First we are recollected in our own souls, then we are drawn to the love of our fellow men, and finally we are lifted up to heaven.[20]

Another Cistercian abbot, Gilbert of Holland, continued Bernard's incomplete series of sermons on the *Song of Songs*.[21] Gilbert is not Bernard's equal, but the love he describes is basically the same. Bernard and William of St. Thierry had not expected to startle their readers with radically new ideas. They hoped to provide illuminating variations on a theme that had been heard in the monasteries for centuries. The other monastic writers of their day hoped for no more.

The main business of the monastery was love of God, but the monks could not ignore the second commandment, to love their neighbor. They knew that they were to love their fellow humans and they expressed that love by showing goodwill to their fellow monks and through acts of charity. Bernard interpreted this kind of love in terms of broad social responsibility. It was love, he claimed, which immersed him in European affairs and forced him to neglect his friends. It was love which required men to take on governmental responsibilities as abbots or bishops when they would prefer a life of solitary prayer.[22] The love of one's fellow man was an acknowledged part of monastic life, although we should recall that practice frequently departed from principle and that even principle did not condemn harshness toward the ungodly: the Jew, the Moslem, the heretic, the unrepentant sinner. In any case, the requirement to love all men was apparently considered a simple matter which needed little study. Through prayer and preaching, one helped others to see and to do the will of God. On a less important level, one ministered to their physical needs.

Friendship was more complicated. The legacy from antiquity, as we have seen, recommended human friendship to the Christian but also suggested that it was a distraction from the love of God. The ambiguity continued. The Cistercian Arnulf of Boyers wrote, "Let the monk have no familiar friend. . . . Let him think as if he alone existed in this universe—only he and God."[23] The Carthusian Guigo in effect rejected friendship when he said that man should love others but not seek any special love for himself.

> Each and every man's love is shared by all men. For individuals ought to love all men. Therefore he who wishes this love to be shown to himself in particular is a thief and thereby becomes guilty against all. . . . So, shout to those who love you: "Cease immediately, miserable men, to admire, revere, or honor me in any way, for I myself am wretched, nor

am I able to bring any help to myself or to you; on the contrary, I need your help."[24]

Bernard himself, who had many close friends, was ambivalent toward friendship. At times he found personal friends an obstacle in his work of loving God and serving all men. "Let us stop this tiring business of exchanging letters," he wrote his friend Oger. "Let us . . . apply ourselves to meditating day and night on the law of the Lord, which is the law of charity."[25] He sometimes seemed to forget, too, the reciprocal character of friendship, as when he wrote Hugh, abbot of Prémontré, "For my part, I am determined to love you whatever you do, even if you do not return my love. . . . I shall cling to you, even against your will; I shall cling to you, even against my own will."[26] If Bernard acted on this extravagant language, he must have seemed a dreadful nuisance to many. He seemed worse than a nuisance to Abelard when he made a show of friendship toward Abelard at the very time he was organizing the opposition against him.

But friendship seems to have flourished among monks despite the misgivings. Their letters are often warm and personal, and Bernard himself was not ashamed to proclaim his friendship for his dead brother Gerard. In his funeral sermon he said:

My soul adhered to his; and we two were made one, not by blood, but by our oneness of mind. We were indeed related by blood, but we were joined more by a community of spirit, a concord of minds, a likeness of manner. We were one heart and one soul. But now a sword has pierced this soul, his and mine, and has

69

cut it in two, sending one part to heaven but leaving
the other here on earth. . . . I do confess that I am
not insensible to suffering; I am terrified by death,
the death of myself and the death of mine. And he
was mine, surely Gerard was mine. Or can I not
claim as mine him who was my brother in blood, my
son in our order, my father in his solicitude for me,
my consort in spirit, my intimate in affection? He is
gone from me. I feel it. I have been cut, and deeply.[27]

Only one twelfth-century monk wrote at length
about friendship, Ailred of Rievaulx, and he lived in
England, not in France. It is true that his ideas found
favor with at least one Frenchman. Peter of Blois, an
ecclesiastical statesman and writer of some repute,
liked them so much that he published as his own a
thinly disguised plagiarism of Ailred's work.[28] But
despite Peter's thievery, Ailred's ideas can be included here only by stretching the geographical limits
of this book. The ideas seem worth the sacrifice.

As a student, Ailred had read Cicero's work on
friendship. Around 1160, when he was 50 years old, he
returned to the subject. Ailred's experiences and his
Christian faith convinced him that Cicero's treatment
was inadequate. Whereas Cicero wrote *On Friendship,*
Ailred's title was *On Spiritual Friendship.* That patience and sensitivity with which monks examined the
movements of their hearts toward God, Ailred turned
to the analysis of love between human friends.

In a conversation with several other monks, Ailred
sets out to explain true friendship. Just as the love of
God appears in various imperfect forms which may

develop into "true" or "perfect" love, so also does friendship have its false or imperfect forms. There are childish and adolescent friendships that are primarily self-centered, based on unstable infatuation. Mature friendship, though, is moved by reason as well as affection.

> When reason declares a man lovable because of his virtue, and at the same time the heart is won over by his charming manner and by the sweetness of his praiseworthy life, then there is love from both reason and affection. And reason is so joined to affection that the love made chaste by reason is made sweet by affection.[29]

Such a love is not an immediate and spontaneous achievement. Rather, friends must seek each other out and must get to know each other's qualities, "For clearly, one must beware the impulse of love which rushes ahead of judgment and which takes away the power of discriminating" (col. 689). The friends must be able to trust each other so that they are utterly secure together. They must have no ulterior motives for their friendship. They must show discretion so that they know when to grant favors to each other and when to ask them, when to console and when to congratulate, and they must be able to correct each other, when necessary, in an appropriate manner, time, and place. And they must show patience, so that each will suffer any adversity for the sake of his friend, even the friend's rebukes. As the two grow close, they demonstrate the inner sweetness of their love with gestures of benevolence; they reveal the secrets of their hearts to each other with growing confidence; they take joy in sharing anything, even in sharing sorrow.

The Christian must love all men, but he cannot be a friend to all. "From them he selects one whom he admits to the secrets of friendship . . . upon whom he generously bestows his affections, to whom he bares his breast, revealing his innermost being, the marrow of his bones, the thoughts and intentions of his heart" (col. 700). And then the two experience the oneness Cicero had spoken of, that "supreme oneness of mind in things human and divine" (col. 680). They are of one heart and mind, united in intention, hoping and praying for each other's salvation, even becoming one in appearance as the expression of one friend's face mirrors the expression of the other's.

The monastic habits of sensitive introspection, of honest self-analysis, and of lucid expression bore unique fruit in Ailred's treatment of friendship. He had no doubts about human friendship. It was no distraction from the love of God; it was a way to reach God. "The friend, adhering to his friend in the spirit of Christ, is made one heart and one soul with him and so rising up through the stages of love to the friendship of Christ, he is, in one kiss, made one spirit with him" (col. 672).

It is a pity that twelfth-century monks, these gifted interpreters of human experience, were never able to do for sexual love what Ailred did for asexual friendship. The celibacy of conscientious monks, of course, meant that the experience was not there to be analyzed. And their ascetic tradition did not allow them to be sympathetic or even attentive students of the sexual experience of others. Sexuality was a danger even to the married. When Bernard wrote letters to married couples, he commonly warned them to love each other, but to love God more.[30]

Not that the monks were completely insensitive to the value of married life. To the monks, the Church was the bride of Christ and the soul loved Christ as the bride loves the bridegroom. Bernard wrote, "There is no way to express more sweetly the affection between the soul and the Word than by calling them bride and bridegroom, for bride and bridegroom share all things, holding back nothing from each other. They have one inheritance, one home, one table, one bed, and even one flesh."[31]

And Peter the Venerable, abbot of Cluny, surely saw value in the love of man and woman. When Abelard died, Peter wrote to Heloise about the last days of her former lover and husband. She had now long been a nun and Abelard a monk, but Peter wrote:

Dear and venerable sister in the Lord, where is he, to whom you were joined first in carnal union but then by the sounder, better bond of divine love? Where is he with whom and under whose direction you have long served the Lord? Now Christ, in your place, even as another you, comforts him in his arms and keeps him safe; and he will restore him to you, through God's grace, at the coming of the Lord, at the voice of the archangel, at the trumpet of God descending from heaven.[32]

Peter could understand love between man and woman, but only a love purged of erotic sexuality.

The modern student of conjugal love, then, will not find his counterpart among twelfth-century monks, for they loved an invisible God and his visible incarnation, long since departed from the world. They wrote for those who would love the transcendent God. But even the most secular student of love is indebted to the monks for their methods, their conclusions, and their ideals. They studied love empirically, by searching their own hearts. How fruitful the method could be was demonstrated by Ailred's analysis of human friendship. What is more, their conclusions about love retain their validity, even for a secular age, for the love of God is not utterly remote from the love of a human person. The monk's God is intangible, inscrutable, beyond complete comprehension, but so also is the human personality. The monk labored hard at his task. The love of God was sweet, but it was achieved only by stages, by conscious and determined effort, by overcoming the obstructions of selfishness, and by expending time and thought in trying to know and become one with the Beloved. These conclusions are timeless and universal. And even if their methods had been faulty and their conclusions false, the monks would still deserve a major place in the history of civilization. They kept alive the belief that the life of love is a viable ideal.

CHAPTER FOUR

The Courts

THE ARISTOCRATIC court was a most unlikely place for love-poetry to flourish. The court was the principal room of a castle, and its main business was war. Most of the castles which dotted Europe were wooden towers with two or three rooms, but the more powerful nobles of France could boast of at least one stone castle, perhaps even one as elegant as that of the counts of Flanders, still standing in Ghent. The weapons and armor of a warrior class shaped the lives of everyone who lived in these castles: the ruling family, the household knights, the clerks, servants, sycophants, and hangers-on. Like wood and stone, leather and steel, marriage was only part of the armory. The history of the courts is one of scheming and fighting to bring yet another castle and the land it dominated under control. The ultimate prize was all of France, and perhaps even more.

The history of these courts is a confusing one, but one can impose an impressionistic pattern on the political maneuvering by dividing France and the twelfth century into halves. In the first half of the century, several dynastic houses competed for domination of the north while several others competed for domination of the south. In the second half of the century, the competition was for all of France, and it had been narrowed down to two families, the Capetians and the Angevins.

Before about 1150, the contenders in the north were the Capetian kings (who controlled the vicinity of Paris), the house of Anjou (called "Angevin"), the house of Blois-Champagne, and, until his death in 1135, Henry I, king of England and duke of Normandy.

In 1100, the Capetian King Philip I had only eight more years to live of a life given largely to pleasure. The only notable conquest of his last years was Bertrade de Montfort, countess of Anjou, for whom he repudiated his wife and antagonized the pope. His son Louis VI—called "The Fat"—inherited his father's corpulence but none of his indolence. During his reign, from 1108 to 1137, he fought countless petty wars against surrounding warriors, some of whom, with no more than a single castle, defied the king for years. His successor, Louis VII, was less impressive. A chronicler remarked about his performance on the Second Crusade, "He was able to do nothing useful, nothing memorable, nothing worthy of France."[1] That judgment is unduly harsh, but Louis VII did not impress his contemporaries, and he has not much impressed posterity.

The Angevins were a tough family of obscure origin that had gradually come to dominate the valley of the Loire. Fulk Rechin, who died in 1109, held his position by keeping a brother locked in a dungeon for 30 years and by having a rebellious son killed. In his last years, he let King Philip take his wife, Bertrade, and even gave the couple a royal welcome when they came to call, but he was less careless of his castles than he was of his wife. His son Fulk V, and even more his grandson, Geoffrey Plantagenet, added to the family possessions. By marrying Mathilda, daughter of Henry I of England, Geoffrey acquired a claim to Normandy that he made good in 1144. By the same marriage he added England to the enormous inheritance of his son Henry. Henry inherited Anjou (with its surrounding counties of Touraine and Maine), Normandy, and England. That young man is known in English history as Henry II, king of England, father of the common law, friend and enemy of Becket, but he was first and foremost an Angevin prince of France.

For a while, it seemed that Blois-Champagne might rival the Capetians and Angevins. The two counties, Blois and Champagne, were ruled separately until 1125 when Hugh of Champagne turned over his lands to his nephew, Thibaut IV, count of Blois. Hugh was forever having trouble with his wives: one deserted him for the crusading hero Bohemond of Antioch; another he simply found increasingly distasteful. Each time, he escaped the unpleasantness attending the annulment by making a pilgrimage to Jerusalem. In 1125, he went for good and left the family's fortunes in the hands of Thibaut, a man of much greater ambition than himself. Thibaut and his brother Stephen were grandsons of William the Conqueror, and they tried to use that inheritance to get not only Normandy but England as well. When Thibaut died in 1152, however, Normandy belonged to the Angevins, and at Stephen's death in 1154 so also did England. In the second half of the century, then, the main contenders in the north were to be the Capetians and the Angevins.

In the south, the competitors were a good deal weaker than in the north. No southern prince had as much control of the towns and petty barons as the Angevins did in the north. But there were several who showed promise. The counts of Auvergne might have fared better had they avoided family squabbles. In 1126, Count William VIII quarreled with his brother the bishop of Clermont and threw him into prison, thus giving King Louis the Fat an opportunity to invade the uplands of Auvergne as a defender of the clergy. Around 1208, another count of Auvergne imprisoned another bishop of Clermont—once again, his brother—and, once again, a royal army appeared. This time, the king kept the better part of Auvergne for his trouble, and the counts of Auvergne were out of the running.

The counts of Toulouse were more powerful, but they could not resist the call to take the cross. For the first half of the century, Count Alphonse-Jourdain withstood incursions from all sides, although at times his enemies occupied Toulouse itself, but in 1148 he died in the Holy Land, as his father and brother had done before him. The princes of Toulouse sacrificed the future of their dynasty for the crusades. Ironically, a few generations later, the homelands of these zealous crusaders would be devastated by a "crusade," the crusade against the Albigensians.

A crusader of a quite different stamp was William IX, count of Poitou and self-styled duke of Aquitaine. When his neighbor the count of Toulouse departed for the first crusade in 1096, William took the opportunity to invade Toulouse. In 1100, he quarreled with a papal legate at Poitiers, and shortly thereafter, as the legate stood near the altar in Poitiers, a rock came hurtling down from the rafters. It missed the legate, but a nearby cleric lay sprawling in a pool of blood. The next year William did leave for the Holy Land, but he returned in a few months, having lost everything to thieves except the headful of memories with which he filled witty, self-mocking verse.

William was a prince and a poet, and his life and his poetry were of the same style, flexible, imaginative, and unorthodox. When he tired of his second wife, he took a viscountess as his mistress and was reproved by an indignant bishop. William told the bishop, who was quite bald, that he would indeed give up his viscountess—on the occasion of the bishop's next haircut. As a prince, William maintained as much order as could be expected in an unruly land, and for twenty years was strong enough to refuse to do homage to King Louis the Fat.

William's son, William X, gave his family's future a new direction when, at his death, he left his daughter and heiress, Eleanor, to the care of Louis the Fat. From

79

his deathbed, Louis arranged for her marriage to his son Louis VII in 1137, and the Capetian family had apparently acquired Aquitaine and a new preeminence in the south. But Eleanor proved to have a mind of her own. She and Louis did not get along. On the Second Crusade, rumor had it that she found consolation with men more worldly than her pious spouse, and in 1152 they separated. The Capetians thereby lost Aquitaine. The Angevins were not slow to find it, for within the year Henry married Eleanor, eleven years his senior. When Henry inherited England two years later, the Angevin Empire had been born, stretching from Scotland to the Mediterranean. In the second half of the century, therefore, the Capetians and the Angevins contended for dominance of all France, and the Capetians were decidedly the underdogs.

The Angevins were more impressive than the Capetians in almost every way. The vigor, the intelligence, and the fearful temper of Henry II made Louis VII seem even more lackluster than he was. Henry's son Richard the Lion-Hearted was known to Christians and Moslems alike as the greatest warrior of his day, while his Capetian contemporary, Philip Augustus (II), avoided battles whenever he could. Richard's brothers Henry and Geoffrey were models of chivalric courtesy and valor. But the Capetians were equipped by nature with crucial assets for an hereditary monarchy: they lived a long time and they had sons. Louis the Fat and Louis VII were both crowned during their fathers' lifetimes. Louis VII failed to produce a male heir for almost thirty years, but in 1165, Philip Augustus was born. News of his birth reached the monks of St.-Germain-des-Prés as they were chanting, "Blessed is the Lord God of Israel, since he has visited and brought salvation to his people," and the monks took it as a good omen.[2]

Philip justified their expectations, for during his long reign, from 1180 to 1223, he learned to be patient in awaiting opportunities and quick to seize them. He died the strongest man in France. He had earned the name "Augustus" by "augmenting" his kingdom. By then, the king of England still held Aquitaine, but he need no longer be called an Angevin. Anjou, as well as Maine, Touraine, and Normandy, had become part of the Capetian inheritance.

The preferred literature of men like these was the *chanson de geste*. Works like the *Song of Roland*, finally put in writing around 1100, described in vivid and endless detail what interested the knight most, war:

Count Roland does not spare himself; he fights with his spear as long as the shaft lasts, but after the fifteenth stroke it shatters and becomes useless. Then he draws his good sword Durendal, he bares the blade, and spurs his horse and charges against Chernuble. He cleaves the helmet glittering with carbuncles, sheers through the steel hood and leather coif, splits the skull and face between the eyes, and carving down through the polished hauberk made of fine mail, halves the whole body all the way to the groin. His sword plunges on, and passing through the saddle covered with beaten

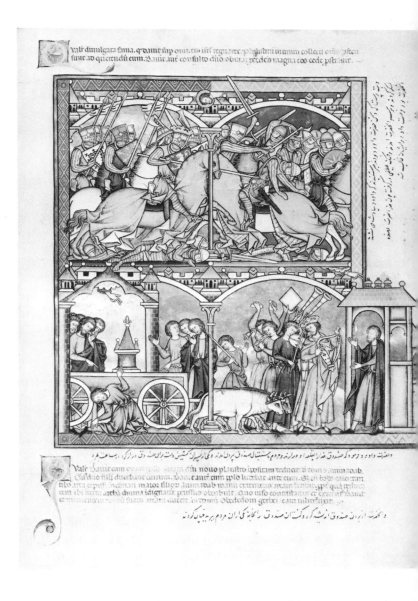

When this thirteenth-century artist portrayed battle scenes and court musicians to illustrate Old Testament stories of King David, he certainly used models from his own day.

Similarly, when portraying the story of David and Bathsheba (Plate 7), he very probably had in mind some contemporary examples of princely lust.

gold, sinks into the horse, severs its spine, grinding through no joint but through solid bone, and Roland hurls down horse and man, dead, on the rich grass of the meadow. Then he says to the corpse: "Wretch, you came here to your sorrow, and you will have no help now from Mahomet! It is not by such scum as you that a battle is won, and won quickly."[3]

Roland has softer emotions, but he does not waste them on women; they are for his fallen comrades and for his beloved sword, Durendal.

It is no surprise that warriors loved stories of war, but it is surprising that about the same time the *Song of Roland* was written, William IX of Aquitaine was composing the following song:

> With the sweetness of the season new
> Burgeon the woods, and birds sing true
> Each in his own special tongue
> Following song's new poetry;
> All should now enjoy that thing
> That man desires most ardently.
>
> From where she dwells, most good and fair,
> Comes no sealed note nor messenger,
> No step forward dare I go,
> My heart can have nor joy or rest
> Until the end I really know
> Whether she be as I request.
>
> Our love proceeds in the same way
> As a branch of hawthorn spray
> That trembles high upon the tree,
> At night exposed to frost and rain,
> Until the morrow, through the leaves,
> The sun shines on the branch again.

I still remember one fine morning
We made an end to all our warring,
So great a gift to me she made,
She gave her ring and all her love:
God, let me live until the day
My hands beneath her mantle move.

For strange rumors let me not care
That part me from my Neighbor Dear
For I know how words behave
With brief speech that spreads increasing,
Let others go and boast their love
We have what we need for feasting.[4]

When Count William wrote this song early in the twelfth century, he was only the first of the Provençal troubadours. Their numbers increased, and before the century was out, love songs were being sung in noble courts not only in northern France, but in Provence, Germany, Italy, Spain, Portugal, and England. The love of man for woman became, for the first time, a favorite theme in European literature.

In the twelfth century, professional warriors in France began to temper their crude and brutal manners with *courtoisie,* or *courtesy,* the refined elegance which was in time to become the ideal of the aristocratic courts of Europe. These knights shared in the increasing wealth of the time and they may have had somewhat more leisure than in earlier days. They profited from the intellectual revival of the century. Though most were called illiterate—that is, they could not read Latin—many were learning to read their vernacular tongues. And faced with flourishing townsmen whose wealth and education challenged the position of the warrior class, they welcomed anything that set them apart from, and above, the pretentious commoners. Their horses, their weapons, their armor, their training made them knights, *chevaliers*. They were warriors who did not work; they owned land and ruled over men; they would have their own style of life to reinforce their claim to superiority, a claim not yet securely fortified by hereditary legal privileges.

Why love-poetry should have become part of this "courtesy" has puzzled scholars for many years. Some have found the origins of troubadour love-poetry in the literary influences coming from Ovid, from Moslem Spain, or from the language of love used by Christian monks. Others have stressed the social and psychological causes: the influence of women in the court (especially with men away for crusades or other wars), the high ratio of men to women in the courts, the psychological immaturity of the troubadours, or the ambivalent state of all men, who see in women both the all-powerful, life-giving mother of their childhood and the small, weak dependent of their manhood. Others have found connections between some of the heresies of the twelfth and thirteenth centuries and troubadour love-poetry.[5] For the purposes of this book, however, the troublesome term *courtly love* and the scholarly debates about it are best avoided. For whatever reason, there was in the courts of twelfth-century France a new interest in love, and that interest gave a new direction to European life and literature.

86

The love songs of the troubadours present no well-defined set of ideas which can be neatly labeled "courtly love." They contain, rather, a "spectrum of attitudes."[6] Some of these attitudes became conventions, not universally accepted but certainly very common, which can be set forth rather simply. The most familiar convention is the suppliant knight "courting" an idealized lady. The lady is beautiful and desirable, but remote; the poet speaks to her as a humble knight, offering his services to her as a vassal to his lord or as a man to his God. His love for her makes him a faithful lover and a better knight, one who will brave all dangers for her favor, but one who is at the same time made humble and gentle in his supplication. The love of the troubadour is mainly a love of desire, not consummation. The mood shifts from the joy the beloved inspires in him to the sorrow he feels because he does not possess her. He wants to win her freely-given love, but his song usually stops short of his receiving it. The concluding mood may be hopeful anticipation or mournful longing, but it is rarely satisfaction.

Examples of these conventions, grown more complex since the time of Count William, can be seen in this song of Bernart de Vantadorn, a troubadour patronized by Eleanor of Aquitaine herself in mid-century:

> Singing is not worth a thing
> if the heart sings not the song,
> and the heart can never sing
> if it brings not love along.

Thus *my* song never can go wrong,
for I to love's use have assigned
my heart, my eyes, my mouth and mind.

I would not have from God the power
to escape my love's disdain,
and if I had no good of her,
but every day she brought me pain,
courageous would I yet remain,
and I would gain much more content
from my pure heart than from lament.

Fools laugh at love whose hearts are stilled
in ignorance, but harm need not befall,
for love is not so quickly killed
unless it is not mutual,
and then it is not love at all,
but only name and form and faking:
there is no love without taking.

. . . .

My dearest hopes grow grand and bold
when fate presents the lovely face
that I most love and must behold,
noble, gentle, true, without a trace
unlovely, and a body sweet with grace.
She could bring salvation to the king;
she has made me rich from nothing.

As deeply as I love I fear,
and nothing causes more dismay
than keeping all her wishes dear.
It seems Christmas every day
her soul-filled eyes turn my way,

> but this they are so slow to do,
> it's months till every day is through.[7]

The ladies addressed in the poems are usually married. Perhaps the troubadours created a "cult of adultery," as some have said. More likely, they were simply interested in love, and in twelfth-century France, love had very little to do with marriage. Through marriage, one acquired wealth and position. Love entered into the bargain more by chance than by design. Moreover, the troubadours and their northern counterparts, *trouvères,* were often men who wished to win favor in aristocratic courts, and the important women of the courts, the ones to be flattered or "courted," were nearly always married. And finally, the troubadours, for whatever reason, liked to sing about the changing emotions of unsatisfied desire, an experience not common in aristocratic marital arrangements. The marriage was accomplished without desire, and afterwards desire was satisfied without delay.

The troubadours, then, were not especially interested in attacking marriage. Rather, marriage, often in the person of a jealous husband, kept intruding into the realm of love. The poets were interested in the flickering emotions of incipient love, and their subject was necessarily suspect to society. To the Christian ascetic, erotic love was the lure of hell. To the secular prince, who could always find women to sate his lust, the love of the troubadours detracted from the real importance of marriage as a means to transfer wealth

89

and power. It also threatened the legacy of his heirs, for a wife who succumbed to the ideas of the troubadours might give her husband another man's bastards for his heirs. Small wonder, then, that the troubadours, somewhat defensively, show distaste for the harsh rules of marriage, which made small allowance for love.

Without drastically changing their society, the troubadours gave to Europe a new set of ideals. Not that they or their audiences entertained a thoroughly consistent set of ideas about love nor that their behavior necessarily conformed to their ideals. They honored constancy between lovers, but were not therefore necessarily constant. They praised gentleness, humility, moderation, and discretion in lovers, but they did not witness an utter transformation in the brutality and coarseness of twelfth-century life. But for all that, something new had been added. A new set of standards was emerging which must have, to some degree, refined and softened the life of the courts. The troubadours suggested some middle ground between the ascetic denial of erotic life and the insensitive acceptance of sexuality as a source of offspring to be sired and pleasure to be seized. Refined erotic love between man and woman, called "true love" or "pure love" or "fine love" by the poets, became something good in itself.

This new interest in love grew in southern France and found expression in the dialect of the area, but it was not long confined to that region or to that tongue. When Eleanor, the granddaughter of William IX, went north as the wife of Louis VII in 1137, her literary tastes went with her, and she passed them on to her children by Louis and by Henry Plantagenet. Henry and Eleanor, apart or together, were the leading patrons of poets in Poitou, Anjou, Normandy, and England. Eleanor's daughter Marie married Count Henry of Champagne in 1159, and while the count's interests inclined him to the company of scholars and to Latin works on religious and historical themes, Marie encouraged some of the outstanding French poets of the day, including Chretien de Troyes. The court in Troyes, which had been visited regularly by St. Bernard only a few years before, now sheltered a patroness of the new secular love poetry, an eventuality which surely would have horrified the stern Cistercian.

The northern writers adopted the troubadours' themes of love and wove them into materials from the past, stories of Troy, of Greece, of Rome, and of King Arthur's court. Besides writing love songs in the manner of the troubadours, they adapted tales of knightly adventure so that the resulting "romances" were lengthy stories not only of adventure but of love as well.

No more than the troubadours did the northern writers have a single notion of love. But like the troubadours they were fascinated by the early stages of love, the single-minded absorption of the lover in the thought of the beloved, the mixed joy and sorrow of new love, the moral purification which turns the lover from any thought of indiscriminate lust. Even more

than the troubadours, they recognized that the claims
of this love often conflicted with society and even with
nature. Too often, society and fate seemed to conspire
to keep lovers apart. Too often, the rules of marriage
raised obstacles between the lovers, or fate drew the
eternal triangle in which at least one must suffer.

Often the conflict between love and social convention produced tragedy. The Celtic story of the fated
love between Tristan and Iseult was well known in the
twelfth century. Tristan was a knight sent by his uncle
King Mark of Cornwall to escort Iseult from Ireland to
be the king's bride. By mistake, Tristan and Iseult
drank the love potion intended for the king and his
bride, and from that moment on, despite Iseult's
marriage to the king, despite the king's waning and
waxing suspicion, the two were fated to be lovers. In
the end, their adulterous love caused their deaths.
From the twelfth century on, Tristan and Iseult were
known in European literature as the symbols of lovers
driven to their own destruction by a love which, for all
its destructiveness, had still a haunting beauty.

Marie de France also found tragic love stories in the
melancholy riches of folklore. The first woman writer
of French literature, she was patronized by Henry II of
England. She told the story, for example, of the knight
who loved his neighbor's wife and she him. Their
homes were separated by a wall which kept them
apart; but they could throw notes back and forth
across the wall, and they could see each other by
standing at their windows. When spring came, the
lady would rise each night to gaze upon her beloved

across the way, and when her husband complained, she told him she rose to hear the song of the nightingale that sang each night in the garden. Perhaps suspecting the truth, her husband snared the nightingale, wrenched off its head, and threw the body on her lap. The love was ended. She sent the dead nightingale to the knight next door, who had it encased in a tiny casket of gold and fine jewels. The lovers saw each other no more, for society preferred marital rights to ennobling love, brutal husbands to gentle lovers.

On the other hand, not all the stories are so somber; the obstacles raised by man or nature are overcome. Marie herself tells tales of lovers who live happily ever after. In one of them, *Lanval,* a vassal of King Arthur repulses the improper advances of the queen for the sake of a fairy maiden whom he loves. The queen gives the king a rather distorted version of the incident, and Lanval is nearly disgraced before the maiden appears to save his good name. Then he and his beloved ride off on a single palfrey, never to be seen again.

In *Eliduc,* another of Marie's tales, the knight Eliduc falls in love with a young princess but is torn between his love for her and his devotion to his wife. When the princess learns that he is married, she falls into a coma and is taken for dead. Eliduc leaves her body, which remains perfectly preserved, with a hermit and visits her every day. His wife becomes concerned about his sadness and, investigating, discovers the princess and is able to revive her. Then the lady, surely the most obliging wife in all literature, retires to a convent so that the lovers can marry. And finally, the claims of love, of secular society, and of religion are perfectly reconciled when the happy couple decide that they too will abandon the world for the monastic life. The triangle of love is purified, and the three lived out their days in holy friendship.[8]

The greatest of the northern writers was Chrétien de Troyes. It was Chrétien who first gave us the story of Lancelot and Guinevere. The romance had been requested by Eleanor's daughter Marie of Champagne, but Chrétien never finished it. Some say he disliked the adulterous theme, and perhaps he did, for he was at pains in his other romances to reconcile love with society. He had little sympathy with the oppressive marriages of convenience, but neither did he care for adultery or promiscuity. He praised mutual love between man and woman, freely given and faithfully preserved, and his stories usually ended with his lovers happily married.

Chrétien's romance *Cligés* is a good place to find his views on love, for, in almost 7000 lines, it takes the reader through two generations of lovers.[9] The story begins with Alexander, the son of the emperor of Constantinople, travelling with his brother Alis to the court of King Arthur. There he falls in love with Soredamors, the sister of Gawain and handmaiden to the queen. Soredamors loves him, too, but they cannot bring themselves to confess their love. Rather, through lengthy, solitary monologues, they puzzle over their emotions, complain of their malady, and yearn for some sign from the other that their love is returned. At one point, Alexander discovers that a shirt he has been given has stitched into it a single golden hair from the head of Soredamors, and he is ecstatic. "He kisses it more than a hundred thousand times, feeling how fortunate he is. . . . All night he presses the shirt in his arms, and when he looks at the golden hair, he feels like the lord of the whole wide world" (p. 112). Alexander knows that the king would give him the hand of Soredamors if he asked, but "he prefers to suffer without her rather than to win her against her will" (p. 120). Finally the queen intervenes. She advises them "to seek no passing gratification in your love; but to be honourably joined together in marriage" (p. 121). They are married, and in due time, Soredamors gives birth to Cligés.

Alexander takes his wife and child back to Greece, where his brother Alis has unfairly taken the title of emperor. Alexander allows him to keep it, with the provision that he never marry and that he make Cligés his heir. In the years that follow, Alexander and Soredamors die, and, contrary to his promise, Alis decides to marry. He arranges to marry Fenice, the daughter of the German emperor, and goes to Cologne with Cligés and a company of knights to escort her to Constantinople. There, Cligés and Fenice first see each other. "The day outside was somewhat dark, but he and the maiden were both so fair that a ray shone forth from their beauty which illumined the palace, just as the morning sun shines clear and red." It was a magic moment. Without a word being spoken, "She handed over to him the possession of her eyes and heart, and he pledged his in turn to her" (pp. 126–27).

And now Fenice confides in her nurse Thessala. "My illness is different from all others; for when I wish to speak of it, it causes me both joy and pain, so happy I am in my distress" (p. 131). Thessala diagnoses the malady at once as love, and the two of them begin to look for a solution to Fenice's dilemma. She loves Cligés but is betrothed to Alis, and she will not give herself to both as Iseult did with Mark and Tristan. "I could never bring myself to lead the life that Iseult led. . . . Who has the heart has the body, too, and may bid all others stand aside" (p. 132). So Thessala prepares a magic potion which will make Alis think he is possessing Fenice when he is really dreaming. The plan works. The marriage is accomplished but Fenice remains a virgin.

To bring the story this far, Chrétien has described a number of battles, and Cligés, like his father, has frequently distinguished himself for his prowess. But the finishing school for the heroes of romance was Arthur's court, so Cligés, trying not to reveal his love, takes his leave of his uncle's wife. He goes to England and further enhances his reputation with deeds of valor, dutifully recounted by Chrétien. Only when he returns, do he and Fenice declare their love to each other, and Fenice reveals that she has preserved her maidenhood. But she will not give herself to Cligés as long as she lives as the wife of Alis.

Once again, Thessala provides a potion. This one makes Fenice appear to be dead. There follow many harrowing complications and close calls, but Cligés finally manages to sneak Fenice from her sepulcher to a secret room in a tower next to an enclosed garden. For over two years, the lovers meet there in secrecy until a knight accidentally discovers them lying in the garden in a nude embrace. The lovers flee to England and, with Arthur's support, are gathering an army to conquer Alis, when word reaches them that Alis is dead. Cligés and Fenice return to Constantinople, are married, and are crowned emperor and empress.

> His mistress he has made his wife, but he still calls her his mistress and sweetheart, and she can complain of no loss of affection, for he loves her still as his mistress, and she loves him, too, as a lady ought to love her lover. And each day saw their love grow stronger: he never doubted her, nor did she blame him for anything (p. 178).

The love poets had very little to say about the growth of consummated love. It should surely endure, like the love of Cligés and Fenice, but Chrétien can say no more than that their love "grew stronger." He might have learned from the monks about the stages of love, about the gradual process of mutual self-revelation, of the erosion of selfishness for the sake of the other. But the lovers in the poetry usually do not consummate their love, or if they do, the story is over. Like the monks, the poets tried to understand the experience of loving, but, like them, they excluded conjugal love, the love which begins rather than ends with sexual union.

Like the monks, however, the poets should be remembered for what they did as well as for what they did not do. The poets of the courts shared an insight which they expressed and preserved, that the passionate love that draws man and woman together in a union of heart and mind, of body and soul, is a thing of value. The notion seems obvious now, but if it was mentioned at all in Christian Europe before the twelfth century, it was flatly rejected. The ascetic tradition of the monks left no room for erotic love. Sexual union was necessary for offspring, but sexual pleasure was lust. No matter whether erotic desire and pleasure were part of an enduring personal union or the distraction of a momentary passion; they were still lust. On the other hand, the warriors of France had used women for their ambitions and for their pleasure, but they had not been much inclined to value the love of one particular woman as an ennobling thing.

The love poets were fascinated by incipient love, that psychic disruption which seemed at once akin to madness and to saintliness, which brought both joy and sorrow to the lover, which inspired in him both passion and reverence, which bestowed upon him unbounded desire and the will to restrain it. They tried to make a place for the love of man and woman amid the values of the day, to shelter gentle, sensitive, and faithful sexual love from the asceticism of the monks and from the ambition and brutal sensuality of the knights.

The poets had some success. Certainly the women welcomed ideas which raised them to be the equal or even the superior of their knightly lovers and "vassals." Some men as well accepted the ideals and made them the sign of an inner aristocracy, one whose status was derived not from birth or wealth, but from a noble heart. And the literary conventions certainly flourished, moving from French literature into German, Spanish, English, and Italian. The insight of the twelfth-century love poets has been preserved and elaborated in the literature of every European language, in every century since then.

But the magic of the poets had its limits. Whatever place love between man and woman had found in European literature, it would have little room in the religious and social realities of Europe for a long time to come. The ascetic tradition did not waver, and the use of marriage as an instrument for conveying wealth and power, rather than love, continued. Love certainly did not displace war as the main interest of the aristocrats, and even the poets sometimes laughed at their own idealization of love. Raimbaut of Orange wrote:

> O would you gain a woman-prize?
> O would you gain the pretty pieces?
> Put menaces in your replies
> When they're discourteous. Be wise,
> And if their impudence increases,
> Then quickly punch them on the nose.
> Rudeness for pride! Yes, take my tip.
> Beat them: they'll come with kissing lip.[10]

For all the talk of love, most knights of the day would probably have preferred songs like those of the troubadour Bertran de Born. Bertran sang of spring, as the others did:

99

> How I like the gay time of spring
> That makes leaves and flowers grow,
> And how I like the piercing ring
> Of birds, as their songs go
> Echoing among the woods.

But his song celebrates the springtime blooming, not of love, but of war:

> I tell you: no pleasure's so large
> (Not eating or drinking or sleep)
> As when I hear the cry: "Charge!"
> Or out of the darkened deep
>   A horse's whinnying refrain,
> Or the cry: "Help! Bring aid!"
> As big and little cascade
>   Into ditches across the plain
> And I see, by the corpses whose sides
> Are splintered, flags furling wide.[11]

The poets rescued erotic love from the monks and the warriors. They did not override the claims of spiritual or secular ambition; they did not extirpate brutish lust; and they left unexplored the unfolding complexities of conjugal love. But in their poetry they created a haven for gentle, faithful, and ennobling erotic love between man and woman.

CHAPTER FIVE

The Towns

EVERYTHING CAME together in the towns:the spices
from the Orient, the grain from the countryside, and
the fish from the sea; the monks, the knights, the
scholars, and the craftsmen; the learning of antiquity
and the frivolity of the moment. All these mingled in
the narrow and noisome streets of the towns. Most of
the towns in France grew up around the castle of some
noble or bishop or around a fortified monastery. Whatever its origins, the town's inhabitants usually went
about their daily business of getting and spending in
the shadow of a church, and the town's protection was
usually in the hands of knights, men in the service of
the ecclesiastical or secular prince who claimed the
town as his own, and who passed a good part of his
time within its walls. Moreover, a town of any size had
its school or schools, where boys and young men

learned their letters and numbers and perhaps even more. In the lecture room, the persevering student heard the legacy of pagan and Christian antiquity read and explained; there and in the churches he learned about the monastic accretions which had enriched that legacy over the centuries. In the streets, amid the cries of the hucksters, the noise of horses and dogs and pigs, he heard the bawdy songs from the tavern and the stories and songs which had been created for the courts but which soon made their way down to the common folk.

The towns themselves survive as testimony to the skill of the craftsmen and merchants who created them, but little survives to tell us about the hearts of their inhabitants. We know their lives were hazardous. The heir of King Louis VI was killed in Paris in a traffic accident: he was thrown to the street when a pig ran beneath his horse.[1] There were the fires and diseases. And in the twelfth century, there were insurrections. Townsmen who found the rule of prince, bishop, or abbot too restrictive for their business interests sought to form "communes" which, while not completely independent, would give the townsmen the right to regulate their own affairs. In 1115, for example, the citizens of Laon rose up against their bishop, an arrogant and avaricious man who was served in his crimes by a burly African slave. During Easter week, the townsmen filled the streets crying "Commune!" They murdered the bishop and his household, they fired the church, and they hunted down and killed the aristocratic families who lived in

Plate 8. The angel driving Adam and Eve from Paradise, sculpture on a church in Clermont-Ferrand. This church was dedicated to "Our Lady," but the viewer was reminded that woman was to blame for much of man's trouble. Here Adam kicks Eve and pulls her hair. Photo courtesy Bildarchiv Foto Marburg.

the city.[2] In 1122, the townsmen of Tours rebelled against the cathedral canons and burned down the church and the castle.[3] In 1147, the abbot of St. Peter's abbey in Sens succeeded in having the townsmen's commune revoked and they killed him for it.[4] In 1155, it was the townsmen of Vézelay against the abbot and monks of the town.[5] And so it went. Local nobles and the king were frequently involved on one side or the other. Sometimes the townsmen succeeded, sometimes not, but they usually paid dearly in blood and silver.

What did love mean to these people? We know that prostitution flourished in the towns. But we can only guess that many men and women grew in natural affection as they raised their families and moved through their daily routines, that the townsmen had their friends, and that perhaps they were especially close when conflict forced upon them a camaraderie akin to that which bound knights together. We know that they were familiar with the basic beliefs of Christianity. They learned them from the clergy, but also from the windows and statuary, those mute sermons which decorated their churches. On the steps of the churches, they saw plays like *Adam,* in which God tells Adam and Eve to love each other, and Adam tells Satan how he loves and fears God.[6]

They understood the obvious requirements of Christian love. Hospitals and leprosaries multiplied in the twelfth century, thanks to the generosity of townsmen as well as of nobles. The townsmen took religion seriously, so seriously that many were willing to risk their lives and property by associating themselves with the ill-defined heresies lumped together under the term Catharism. These heresies were most common in the south, but they could be found all the way to the Rhine and beyond.

Townsmen apparently entertained mixed feelings about women. They built churches in honor of "Our Lady," but on a more practical level, they were little inclined to idealize love or women. Anyone who saw the play *Adam* heard the first husband bitterly reproach Eve for misleading him. In the fabliaux, rather crude stories relished by townsmen, women are commonly portrayed as self-serving and deceitful. *The Wife of Orléans,* for example, was probably known in the twelfth century.[7] This wife of a merchant of Orléans has a young scholar for a lover. The husband grows suspicious, tells his wife he is going on a trip, but returns at night disguised as her lover. She sees through the disguise, but tells him to hide in the attic lest her husband find him. She then tells the servants to defend their master's honor from the rogue upstairs, and while they are thrashing him and throwing him on a trash heap, she has her rendezvous with her lover. The next day, the bruised husband comes home well content that his wife is an utterly faithful woman who knows how to handle young lechers. The tale is typical in that the townsman is victimized by a self-indulgent cleric and by an unfaithful woman.

Whereas the townsmen have left us little about their thoughts on love, the scholars who lived among them have left us a great deal. As in most centuries, the intelligentsia's mastery of the written word gives them a disproportionately large role in later histories. We know what they read, what they wrote, and even some of what they thought in their private moments.

In the early twelfth century, urban schools replaced monastic schools as the main centers of education. The students who went beyond the rudiments and the men who taught them were clergy, but their interests were much more varied than those of the monks, whose only real business was the internal ascent to God. The students who flocked to the schools provided by bishops and by chapters of canons planned to be men of affairs and men of learning, a combination much more common among clergy in the twelfth century than in the recent past. The students, the teachers, and the alumni who became abbots, bishops, popes, and ministers to secular and ecclesiastical princes formed a special intelligentsia within twelfth-century France. Drawn from all social classes, they were one in their Latin learning, in their celibacy, and in their sacred orders.

Most of the urban schools remain unknown, but some became famous, usually through the presence of a respected master. In the Loire valley, Tours and Orléans were distinguished for their schools. The cathedral school of Chartres was blessed with at least one outstanding master, Bernard of Chartres. To the northeast, Anselm had already brought fame to Laon when the rebellious townsmen burned down their cathedral in 1115. His student William of Champeaux attracted other students to Paris. One of those students, the brilliant young Abelard, so humiliated his master that William retired to a monastery. William's withdrawal from the world is suspect since the monastery he founded for the occasion, St. Victor's, was right outside the walls of Paris, and since he stayed there only a few years, but the incident laid the foundation for the greatness of Paris. In 1115, Hugh came to St. Victor, and together with Abelard, who taught at the chapter school of Ste. Geneviève and at the cathedral school of Notre Dame, he made Paris the intellectual center of Europe. Hugh of St. Victor died in 1141, Abelard in 1142, and a chronicler mourned the passing of "these two lights among the Latins."[8]

Like the monastic schools, the urban schools taught the seven liberal arts: grammar, rhetoric, dialectic (logic), arithmetic, geometry, astronomy, and music. The urban schools, however, were more thoroughgoing in their treatment of the arts and were less inclined to subordinate learning to the personal quest for God. Grammar and rhetoric involved the study of the authors of antiquity, pagan and Christian. In effect, they were the study of Latin prose and poetry, of history, of ethics, of theology, and even a smattering of law. The students, and even more the teachers, were familiar with the legacy of antiquity and with its wide variety of ideas on love and friendship. Dialectic, based mainly on Boethius' translation of parts of Aristotle, gave the scholars a tool for understanding and classifying the ideas they gleaned from the legacy. The "scientific" parts of the liberal arts, also based on the writings of the ancients, were pursued with only slightly less enthusiasm than the literary and logical studies, for the study of creation revealed the art of the creator. Whereas the monastic schools taught what was needed for the personal ascent to God, the urban schools made intellectual inquiry a way of life, and they sought to include all knowledge in their inquiries. "Learn everything," wrote Hugh of St. Victor: "You will see afterwards that nothing is superfluous. A skimpy knowledge is not a pleasing thing."[9]

Like the monks, the urban scholars learned from the ancients, but they were less deferential. Their thought was always based on faith, but they were more aggressive in dealing with the Bible, the Fathers, and the ancient pagans. They put questions to the ancients, they rearranged the texts, they tested one authority against another. Their reliance on antiquity as well as their new self-confidence can be seen in the famous statement of Bernard of Chartres, who said that he and his contemporaries had seen further than the ancients, but only because they were dwarfs sitting on the shoulders of giants. The monks sat at the feet of the ancients; the schoolmen sat on their shoulders. The learning of the urban schools was, then, more comprehensive than that of the monasteries, it was pursued more systematically and aggressively, and it was more commonly treated as an end in itself. When the century was over, the schoolmen had added little that was new, but they had performed the task at hand: mastering the legacy from the past.

The schoolmen learned much from the methods of lawyers. For centuries, students of canon law (church law) had been compiling collections of papal pronouncements, conciliar decrees, statements of the Fathers, and the like. From the ninth century on, the collections were usually organized topically, with the clear implication that authorities that seemed to disagree on a given topic needed to be interpreted and reconciled. Theological and legal questions were intermingled, and when twelfth-century theologians and philosophers put together their *Sentences,* or summaries of knowledge, they borrowed freely from the substance and the style of the legal writers. Abelard dramatized the usefulness of logic in reconciling the opinions of the ancients by compiling a list of questions and quoting authorities that seemed to take opposing sides on each question. The need of reconciliation was obvious, and the next step was taken by Peter Lombard in his *Sentences,* a comprehensive and systematic survey of existing theological knowledge, in which the author used logic to interpret and explain wherever possible, just as scholars of jurisprudence were doing.

In works as comprehensive as these, love was discussed within the broad context of reality. In the Lombard's *Sentences,* the first book is on God and the Trinity. There the reader finds lengthy discussions of the role of love within the Godhead. The second book· is on the creation of corporeal and spiritual reality, with discussions of the creation of man and woman, of their sin, and of the implications of that sin for the relationship between man and God and in the sexual generation of mankind. The third book is on the Incarnation, with discussions of the "new law," the law of love. Here Peter considers the requirement that man love God above all things and his neighbor as himself. He inquires into the nature of that love; he asks whether we are to love all men in the same way, whether we should love friends more than enemies, relatives more than strangers. He discusses love as one of the three main virtues, faith, hope, and love. And in the fourth book, on the sacraments, he discusses marriage at great length. Throughout, he borrows freely from the ancient Fathers and takes his definition of marriage from the law of pagan Rome (i.e., the union of a man and a woman joined together in single way of life). Throughout, he uses logic to interpret those ancients: confronted with the statements of two Fathers, one saying relatives are to be loved more than enemies and another saying that all men are to be loved equally, he argues that we love all men equally, in the sense that we will the same good for them—salvation; we love relatives more than enemies in the sense that we feel a stronger affection for them.[10]

Besides the many schoolmen who wrote comprehensive books of *Sentences*, others chose no less comprehensive but very different forms of expression. Some showed a taste for long allegorical poems in which love appears among the characters. Around mid-century, Bernard Silvestris, an alumnus of Chartres teaching at Tours, composed *The Totality of the World (De universitate mundi)*, a poetic account of the origins of the universe. In this work, Neoplatonic figures like Mind, World-Soul, and Nature go about the formation of the natural order and of mankind. Another master, Alain of Lille, later composed elaborate works, part poetry, part prose, in which Love appears as the servant of a personified Nature—a servant, albeit, in need of restraint, not so trustworthy as Nature's handmaiden Chastity.

The breadth of their view kept the schoolmen from treating love as an isolated or narrow part of human experience. Love was all-pervasive. Love was the very life of the Trinity and it bound together God and his creation. Peter Lombard said that love was the Holy Spirit himself; by that same love the Father and Son loved each other; by that same love God loved his creation, and especially rational man; by that same love man loved God and his neighbor.[11] Alain of Lille saw love almost as Boethius had, as one face of nature, nature which bound all things together. Addressing an apostrophe to Nature, he says:

> Oh peace, love, virtue, regimen, power,
> Order, law, end, way, leader, origin,
> Life, light, splendor, image, figure,
>   Rule of the world![12]

So great was love, said Hugh of St. Victor, that in the Incarnation it had drawn God down from heaven and lifted man up from earth. So mighty was its strength, that God was bound and man was freed—to that extent was God humbled and man exalted.[10]

Similarly, the writings of the schoolmen gave a more balanced picture of love between man and woman than did many of their contemporaries. The Cathari, like the Manichaeans centuries before, flatly condemned marriage and procreation as evils. The monks, while not condemning procreation, were little given to reflecting on its value. Laymen too often thought of love as a lust to be indulged or as a means of political and economic advancement and courtly poets fled from harsh realities into a world of romantic fantasy.

The schoolmen affirmed the goodness of marriage and procreation. Alain of Lille hailed nature as the "genetrix of things."[14] Bernard Sylvestris went so far in his enthusiasm for the reproductive powers of nature as to address a hymn of praise to the male sexual organs, thus concluding a work said by one scholar to be "bathed in the atmosphere of a fertility cult, in which religion and sexuality mingle."[15] And all the schoolmen accepted marriage as a sacrament whose main purpose was procreation. Against the laymen's habit of exploiting women, the schoolmen reaffirmed the longstanding belief that marriage must be monogamous and indissoluble, requirements which could only serve to raise women above the level of concubinage. And the masters of Paris gave generously to provide dowries for prostitutes who wished to reform and marry.

However ineffective their opinions may have been in changing society, the schoolmen were unanimous in agreeing that love must be freely given, and that no one could be forced to marry against his or her will. A marriage was made, they said, not by agreements between families, not by priests, not by rituals in the church, but by the free consent of the couple, and it was confirmed by their sexual union. The marriage in a cathedral before a bishop, with all the trappings of a princely ceremony, was no more valid, no more a sacrament, no more a marriage, than was the private commitment made on a spring day between a young man and woman alone in a meadow. The maid in the meadow might later regret the absence of witnesses if her husband simply denied that he had made any such commitment, but in the eyes of God, the schoolmen said, the couple were married. Similarly, no amount of extravagant ritual could make a marriage where either man or woman withheld free consent.

On the other hand, the schoolmen condemned the misuse of sexual powers. Like their pagan and Christian masters of antiquity, they valued moderation and order. When they condemned immoderate and inordinate indulgence of the appetites, and especially of the sexual appetite, they spoke for Seneca no less than for St. Paul. Alain of Lille gave poetic expression to the opinion of all the schoolmen when, in his *Complaint of Nature*, he has Nature complain against homosexuality and the other "unnatural" vices of man. The union of man and woman was the sacramental symbol of the union of Christ and his Church, spiritual in the consent of wills, physical in the joining of bodies. Like the union of Christ and his Church, marriage should be faithful, fruitful, and indissoluble. In this way, human sexual love was integrated into the entire framework of divine providence and human society.

Comprehensiveness, balanced judgment, logical precision, familiarity with the ancients, all these were the marks of men of reason and learning. But the schoolmen were also vulnerable to the occupational hazard of their craft: an insensitivity to experience, an inattentive neglect of empirical data. They reclaimed the wisdom of antiquity, they analyzed it and restructured it into elaborate and comprehensive explanations of God and his universe, but they added little of substance. They were not as responsive to the quiet movements of the soul as were the monks or to the powerful erotic passions of the heart as were the courtly writers. Neglecting experience, they did not understand as well as others such things as the mutuality of love, the growth of love through successive stages, and the value of erotic love.

Mutual love was certainly not an unfamiliar idea to the schoolmen. They knew well the ancient treatises on friendship. It was a favorite subject for schoolroom exercises in poetry and letter-writing. But against this familiarity were working Christian ideals that distracted twelfth-century scholars from the reciprocal character of friendship, just as they had distracted Cassian centuries before. The Christian distrust of erotic love, for example, was frequently at the heart of their praise of friendship. The clerical scholars contrasted friendship with *sevus amor*, violent and passionate love. The main value of friendship for these men was that it was rational and pure of erotic passion.

Perhaps even more subtly eroding the value of mutual love was the Christian emphasis on disinterested love. Peter Abelard argued that a Christian should love God without any hope or expectation of being rewarded or loved in return. The value of love was in the unilateral action of the lover; the response of the beloved added nothing. Love was therefore the act of an individual, not a relationship between two persons. Peter Lombard did not go quite so far, but he too placed little value on the mutuality of love. Basing his discussion on the biblical requirement to love God above all things and our neighbor as ourselves (Matt. 22:39), as well as on the requirement to love our enemies (Matt. 5:44), Peter asked whether it was better to love friends or enemies. He could not decide, but he leaned toward the opinion that it was better to love enemies since that was more difficult than to love friends. The *difficulty*, the element of self-sacrifice, seemed to have greater value than reciprocity in love.[16] Similarly, the mutuality of conjugal love was rarely emphasized in scholastic treatments of marriage. In taking as their model the unilateral benevolence of God, the schoolmen characteristically neglected their own belief that God had taken great pains not only to show his love, but to win man's love in return.

The schoolmen had little to say about growth in love. They would on occasion refer to the stages of love, but they rarely developed them with the insight of monastic writers. And as for erotic love, it was simply a snare. That marriage was good, that man and wife should love each other, that their marriage should include carnal union, these principles they never doubted. But erotic passion was evil. The adage appears again and again: the ardent lover of his own wife is an adulterer.[17] The main purposes of marriage were to procreate and to save man and woman from fornica-

caſtratuſ habenſ deſpouſauit ſibi u/
xorem. Jua prior conditioni renun/
tianſ tranſtulit ſe ad altum. ꝗ illi nup
ſit. Jue cui prius deſponſa fuit repe
tit eam. ｈ ic primum queritᵉ an
contugium poſſit ēē. int̄ uouenteſ.
ｓ eđo an liceat ſponſe a ſponſo diſce
dere ꝛ alii nubere. ｑ uod uero uo
uenteſ matrimonia contrahe non
poſſint multiſ auctoritatibꝫ pbatur.
Jn concilio namꝗ cartagineñſi. cap̄.
·c·iiij. ſtatutum inuenitur de uiduiſ
qui poſt pfeſſam continentiam ꝑiua/
ricate ſunt. Hupcias elegerint exorᵗcernᵗ

Plate 9. This manuscript of Gratian's Decretum shows the kind
of problem which occupied lawyers: The man on the left was
betrothed to the lady, but he had taken a vow of celibacy and she
had married another. Now he claims that she should honor her
betrothal to him. What are the rights of each party? This
legalistic approach to marriage characterized theologians as well
as lawyers. Source: Corpus Christi College, Cambridge, Ms. 10,
fol 268r to C. 27. Photo courtesy The Courtauld Institute.

tion. There were many other lesser goods associated with marriage, but the shared experience of erotic love was not one of them.

Since the line between schoolmen and monks cannot be drawn with precision, there were schoolmen who escaped some of these characteristic limitations. Not surprisingly, the canons regular of St. Victor, men who tried to combine the lives of scholar and monk, cannot easily be classified. Richard of St. Victor, for example, was acutely sensitive to the meaning of mutual love. The inner life of the Trinity, in which each divine person loved the others, showed the epitome of love. "It is proper to true and intimate love," he wrote, "that it bring about, even in persons between whom there is diversity, the same will and the same non-will."[18] This kind of love could not be one-sided, because the persons of the Trinity were equal, each one giving and receiving in mutual love. This kind of love unified persons, even to the extent of that mysterious unity of the Trinity.

Similarly, Richard showed greater interest in the growth of love than most schoolmen. He described the four stages of "violent love" through which the soul seeking God passes in this life.[19] The soul is first "wounded" with love, then captured, then exalted in an ecstatic union with God where the ordinary operations of the soul are suspended. Finally it is returned to terrestrial life to live in Christ-like submission to God until death. Richard displayed the psychological perception characteristic of the monks when he described these stages. He also considered the meaning of these stages for love between humans. He made the unusual concession that "among human affections, conjugal love should hold first place," but like the monks and schoolmen, his interest is elsewhere.[20] He conceded that conjugal love can manifest the first or "wounding" stage of love, in which the lover experiences recurring but not immobilizing psychic disruptions, but it should not be allowed to reach the single-minded preoccupation of "capturing love." It could not promise the ecstatic "excess" or "alienation" of the mind. And it lacked the transforming power to turn the souls into the humble image of Christ which, having tasted divinity, is willing nonetheless to live out its days on earth in submission to God's will and in the service of others. That there might be *analogous* stages in the love between man and woman was a possibility Richard did not explore.

Some schoolmen, then, might capture the insights of the monastic tradition. They were less likely to recognize the values of the courtly writers. Even those who seemed almost pagan in their approval of the generative power of nature had nothing to say about the value or the ennobling power of erotic love between man and woman. Had Abelard's life been different, he might have given erotic love a place in Christian thought. Certainly he was equipped for the task. The breadth of his learning and the incisiveness of his mind were beyond question. Then, in his late thirties, he seduced the young Heloise, only to find, as he later wrote her, that "I loved you beyond measure and longed to hold you forever."[21] His autobiography and their letters attest their single-minded absorption in each other. He wrote love songs instead of philosophy, and neither he nor Heloise showed much concern even for the child that was born of their love. The magnitude of that love, thrown up suddenly like a mountain amid the Christian landscape, might have forced Abelard to rebuild his intellectual structures around it, a new feature of the terrain giving a new complexion to all the old landmarks. But the dominating event of his life came to be not his love for Heloise but his castration, the worst of that "history of calamities" he called his life. Abelard the schoolman and lover became Abelard the monk. "There are eunuchs who have been so from birth, and there are eunuchs who have been made eunuchs by men, and there are eunuchs who have made themselves eunuchs for the kingdom of heaven" (Matt. 19:12). Abelard was only the second of these, but he tried to live the life of the last.

On the other hand, perhaps the castration made no difference. For both before and after, neither Heloise nor Abelard ever wavered from the opinion of pagan and Christian ancients that the true philosopher should be celibate, living above the concerns of the flesh. Neither doubted that sacrificing self was the greatest expression of love: Abelard said man should be willing to give up his own salvation for the love of God; Heloise offered to be Abelard's concubine or to give him up completely out of her love for him. Both were harsh in their condemnation of erotic pleasure. Heloise the nun could not shake off the memory of pleasures shared; her reputation for chastity was, she said, based on hypocrisy. But that her desires were evil in God's eyes she did not doubt. She merely treasured Abelard's love more than God's, or so she told her former lover and husband, heaping coals on the old monk's tonsured head.[22] Molded by Plato and St. Paul, by Seneca and St. Jerome, the landscape of twelfth-century thought was too rigid; if erotic love was to find a place, it must be in the fabled lands of the romances.

Abelard, Peter Lombard, Hugh of St. Victor, Alain of Lille, these well-known schoolmen were only the most visible of the large class of clerical intelligentsia. That group was a mixed bag. Many were less successful, less reverent, less serious than those honored by posterity. In their leisure—leisure resulting from position and wealth or from unemployment and poverty—they indulged tastes which appear less often in the formal treatises of the masters. They had the same Latin learning, the same sharp minds, the same broad view of God's creation; but in their lives and in their literary amusements, love appears in forms different from those found in the serious treatises.

Many found chastity an unbearable burden. Alain of Lille wrote that "of those who follow Venus's 'grammar,' some choose only the masculine gender, others only the feminine, yet others both."[23] Homosexuality seems to have flourished, encouraged perhaps by the tensions of a celibate, male society and by the models of pagan antiquity. Prelates as well as scholars wrote love poems to boys, and the moralists' condemnations of sodomy increased as the century progressed.[24] Many succumbed like Abelard to the beauty of women. Students and scholars who went from town to town grew in number faster than the remunerative positions they sought. They often took consolation in loose living and ribald literature.

These wandering scholars produced a body of Latin poems called "Goliardic" verse after the mythical poet Golias. They sang in the twelfth century, as they do today, the perennial song of the student:

> Let's put away our studies:
> Foolishness is sweet;
> And let's gather in the joys
> Of youth's early heat;
> Seriously to study
> For old age is meet.
>   Swiftly our life passes
>   When in study spent
>   To play in wantonness
>   Early youth is meant.[25]

The sentiments of an older, more sophisticated, and more cynical student were spoken by another writer known only as the Archpoet:

> Down the broad way do I go
>   Young and unregretting,
> Wrap me in my vices up,
>   Virtue all forgetting,
> Greedier for all delight
>   Than heaven to enter in;
> Since the soul in me is dead,
>   Better save the skin.
>
>   . . . .

Sit you down amid the fire,
Will the fire not burn you?
To Pavia come, will you
Just as chaste return you?
Pavia, where Beauty draws
Youth with finger-tips,
Youth entangled in her eyes,
Ravished with her lips.[26]

Equally irreverent was the poem describing a council of nuns held in their convent at Remiremont.[27] The nuns begin with readings, not from the Bible, but from Ovid, and then move on, not to hymns, but to love songs. Invoking the name of Love, god of all things, they debate whether they should accept knights as lovers or only clerics as they have done in the past. The argument goes clearly in favor of the clergy, whose wisdom, discretion, and generosity are praised on all sides. The council ends by calling down an elaborate curse on those who accept knights as lovers. Their sorrows will be perpetual unless they repent, spurn the laymen, and give themselves only to clerics.

The audience for whom these works were created must have been especially pleased with the *Treatise on Love* by Andreas Capellanus (Andrew the Chaplain).[28] Writing in Latin, the language of the clergy, Andreas modelled his work on that of Ovid, but his raw material was drawn from twelfth-century France. Andreas presented the work as a letter to his young friend Walter who had been importuning Andreas for advice about love. Andreas obviously was a man familiar with these matters and he finally consented.

In the first book, Andreas defines and describes love. "Love is a certain inborn suffering derived from the sight of and excessive meditation upon the beauty of the opposite sex, which causes each one to wish above all things the embraces of the other and by common desire to carry out all of love's precepts in the other's embrace" (p. 28). Andreas clearly knew the fashions of the courts. After some preliminary discussions, Andreas provides a number of sample conversations, showing how a commoner, a nobleman, and a high nobleman (who is also a cleric) might approach women of those classes. Then he discusses such matters as the love of clergy, nuns, peasants, and prostitutes and the role of money in love. Throughout, love and marriage are two entirely different—and incompat ible—things.

In the second book, Andreas explains how love can be retained or diminished. He reviews some cases which are purported to have been decided in "courts of love" presided over by some of the ladies of the day: Countess Marie of Champagne, Queen Eleanor of Aquitaine, Viscountess Ermengarde of Narbonne, Countess Isabelle of Flanders. He concludes with the "Rules of Love," which, he says, were provided by the "King of Love." This famous list includes such dicta as: Marriage is no real excuse for not loving; every lover regularly turns pale in the presence of his beloved; he whom the thought of love vexes eats and sleeps very little; and the like (pp. 184-86).

In the final book, however, Andreas rejects the contents of the first two books. He tells Walter that although he has consented to give him the instruction he asked, Walter would be much the wiser to ignore it.

> Read this little book, then, not as one seeking to take up the life of a lover, but that, invigorated by the theory and trained to excite the minds of women to love, you may, by refraining from so doing, win an eternal recompense and thereby deserve a greater reward from God (p. 187).

Andreas reviews, with remarkable thoroughness, all the arguments against love, concluding with an equally thorough diatribe against women. Andreas finally entreats Walter to "accept this health-giving teaching we offer you, and pass by all the vanities of the world, so that when the Bridegroom cometh to celebrate the greater nuptials . . . you may be prepared to go forth to meet him with your lamps filled" (p. 211).

Many scholars have taken the treatise of Andreas to be the serious and almost official statement of the "system of courtly love." In this view, Andreas was naive and a trifle foolish. The opinion is now gaining ground that if anyone is naive or foolish, it is those who were taken in by the satire of a sophisticated twelfth-century cleric. Andreas was a man who knew the fashions of the courts, the tastes of monks, the manners of townsmen, and the interests of the schoolmen. Taking love between man and woman as his subject, he wrote a treatise in the manner of the schoolmen, systematic and comprehensive; but he wrote more for the amusement than for the instruction of his fellow clerics.

In the first two books, Andreas plays upon the ideals of religious and secular life; but the sordid realities of his society keep intruding. Surely, "one can find nothing in the world more desirable than love, since from it comes the doing of every good thing and without it no one would do anything good in the world" (p. 72). Surely a lover should possess every virtue (pp. 59–61). But these delicate principles wither in the hands of the seducer. The old man can argue that since he has developed gentlemanly virtues he deserves the lady's favor, the young man that only her love will enable him to become virtuous (pp. 39–43). If the lady hesitates because of the immorality of adulterous dalliance, the seducer responds in a classic vein, that if she were really interested in morality, she would be praying in a convent rather than flirting in a court. Better to be an honest adulteress than a hypocritically faithful wife. Moreover,

> God cannot be seriously offended by love, for what is done under the compulsion of nature can be made clean by an easy expiation. Besides, it does not seem . . . proper to class as a sin the thing from which the highest good in this life takes its origin. . . . Again, one's neighbor feels no injury from love—that is he should feel none (pp. 109–12).

If the lady refers to her suitor's wife, he merely states flatly that love and marriage are incompatible, although he feels "such affection for her as a husband can" (p. 116). Here is the seducer's eternal appeal to nature and love, to the harmlessness of it all, and his assurance that his wife doesn't—indeed cannot—understand him.

A more aggressive line is offered by a high nobleman to a high noble lady. He explains that there are two kinds of love, "pure love," which "goes as far as the kiss and the embrace and the modest contact with the nude lover, omitting the final solace," and "mixed love," which "culminates in the act of Venus." Being a high-minded gentleman, the suitor prefers pure love, though he declines to disparage mixed love. In any case, he urges the lady to decide, not whether to love or not, but whether it will be pure or mixed love (pp. 122–23). Her decision will apparently not be final, however, for later in the book, Andreas offers his opinion that a lady who has agreed to practice pure love cannot properly refuse to move on to mixed love if her lover persists (p. 167). (With peasant women, Andreas advises, all this is unnecessary. A little flattery and a little force will do the trick [p. 149].)

Love got with money is not love, for "real love comes only from the affection of the heart and is granted out of pure grace and genuine liberality" (p. 144). On the other hand, says Andreas, quoting Ovid, "I know from my own experience that when poverty comes in, the things that nourish love begin to leave, because 'poverty has nothing with which to feed its love'" (p. 30). And generosity, that virtue highly praised by courtly writers who depended on the largesse of their patrons, could not be practiced by a poor man.

The ladies do not escape Andreas' wit. When he presents the most renowned ladies of the day as presiding over courts of love, recommending adultery, and agreeing that love and marriage are incompatible, his judgment on their morals seems obvious. It is a common poetic theme that women are "the cause and origin of everything good" (p. 108), but in his sample dialogues, Andreas suggests that one can go too far in idealizing women. When a lady rejects a clerical suitor because clerics are indolent and gluttonous, the cleric replies, with greater candor than tact, that no one is lazier than a woman, no one more a slave to the belly (pp. 126–29). As for nuns, Walter should completely avoid them. Their seduction is a great crime in the eyes of God and man, yet no one is more easily seduced (pp. 142–44).

The commoner who would mimic the style of the noble lover is distinguished mainly for his tenacity. He is not even discouraged when a noble lady observes that "your calves are fat and roundly turned, ending abruptly, and your feet are huge and immensely spread out so that they are as broad as they are long" (p. 57).

Even the clergy for whom Andreas writes are invited to consider the contrast between the ideals and the realities of their lives. As a man of learning, the cleric cannot resist displaying his dialectical skills even in the midst of a seduction. He begins, "Now I shall prove to you that you cannot properly deprive me of your love." He then marshals syllogism after syllogism, finally arriving at his triumphant conclusion: "Therefore if you find that my character is good you do wrong in denying me your love" (p. 88). Elsewhere, the cleric decides to enlighten his lady about the consequences of women's reaching puberty at an earlier age than men. The lady declines to be instructed in physiology, and her pedantic suitor grumbles that "to have some instruction in physiology and science cannot hurt the goodness of anybody" (pp. 118–21). Andreas concedes that by reason of his high calling, a cleric should keep himself from love, but instruction is provided nevertheless. The clergy are likely to succumb to love "because of the continual idleness and the great abundance of food" in their lives (pp. 141–42).

In the final book, Andreas begins with the traditional arguments against love, but as he warms to the subject, he takes on the fanaticism of the monastic misogynist. The exhaustive list of women's vices, each explained in detail, cannot be reproduced here. An abbreviated version is that all women are avaricious, miserly, envious, slanderous, greedy, gluttonous, fickle, deceitful, disobedient, arrogant, proud, vainglorious, dishonest, drunken, loud-mouthed, indiscreet, wanton, unfaithful, and superstitious. This triumph of summarization applies equally well to all women; there are no exceptions.

In his conclusion, Andreas comments blandly that his book "will if carefully and faithfully examined seem to present two different points of view" (p. 211). Generations of careful and faithful readers have indeed found these two points rather obvious. There is also, though, a single point of view which gives unity to the book. It is the point of view of the urbane and sophisticated cleric, whose tastes have been shaped by the classical satirists and whose life has led him through monasteries, towns, and courts.

The lives of the townsmen who bought and sold remain obscure. We know little of what love meant to them. But their labors created the environment for an articulate, clerical intelligentsia of wide experience who described love with care and proportion. The failures of these scholars were substantial. They neglected the mutuality of love, the growth of love, and the value of erotic love. They condemned erotic passion because its fierce energies numbed the intellect and obscured the pattern of priorities which they defined in their treatises. Still, their achievements were also substantial. Their judgments were precise and well balanced even when their lives lacked focus and moderation. In the satiric literature of their leisure, they recognized their own excesses as well as others'. They preserved, clarified, and developed the legacy from antiquity. They refused to treat the different forms of love as isolated phenomena, but tried to integrate them into a single understanding of reality. They were not successful—no one has been yet—but they made some progress toward reconciling the conflicting claims of God, nature, and man, claims voiced in the name of love.

The towns were the citadels of intellect and reason. There, all ideas met and jostled one another. The style of the towns was already beginning to change the rest of society, but there was still a difference. In the monasteries, the rule was silence; the monk was to be left alone with God and his own thoughts. In the courts, great issues were settled by combat; the knight's fortunes lay in the force of his blows and the strength of his armor. But in the towns—in the markets and in the schools—a man needed to explain himself. The shrewdness of his mind and the quickness of his tongue could make him rich, powerful, learned, or perhaps all three. Among the monks, the poets, and the courtiers of twelfth-century France, one could find originality, sensitivity, and literary grace. But the intellect and wit of the towns provided the century with what would have otherwise been lacking: wide learning, logical precision, breadth of vision, and a sense of proportion.

CHAPTER SIX

The Varieties of Love

THE HISTORIAN'S lot is to make generalizations and then apologize for them. They mask the variety of life. I have already explained that "France" is a very imprecise term to use when speaking of the twelfth century. A similar warning and apology must be made for grouping people under the headings "monasteries," "courts," and "towns." These were not sharply divided entities. Many monks had been raised in aristocratic courts and continued to frequent them. Scholars like Alain of Lille and princes like Count William of Nevers became monks. And everyone passed through the towns. I can only say that despite this intermingling, there were still differences recognized and expected by contemporaries. A townsman aping an aristocrat, a nobleman who seemed too monkish, a scholar playing the courtier, a monk with a sharp eye for a bargain—all these were fair game for ridicule. Just as there was a difference between France and Germany despite the obscurity of the line between them, so also were there universally recognized differences among monasteries, courts, and towns. ﹀

The "twelfth century" is also a generalization. Not only are its boundaries hard to define (the new year began on different dates in different parts of France), but it was not static. Life was changing rapidly in that century, and men knew that it was. Toward the end of the century, arrogant young scholars spoke of themselves as "moderns" who had already mastered and were now surpassing the wisdom of the ancients.

As the twelfth century passed into the thirteenth, the attention enjoyed by love and literature passed to logic and law. The passion for these studies, just appearing in 1100, grew stronger, fed by the influx of Aristotelian works coming into Europe from Arab sources in Spain and Sicily and by the needs of organized society. The study of logic and law flourished in the universities, even among theologians and philosophers, for scholastic philosophy can be fairly considered an amalgam of logic and law. Moreover, schoolmen trained in these disciplines rose high in the service of lay and ecclesiastical princes. The centralization of the Church under the popes and of principalities under rulers like Philip IV of France was the work of logic and of law. All this certainly brought the benefit of greater order to European life and thought, though at the price of less variety.

Not that love or writing about love disappeared. The

lyric love poetry of the troubadours and the romances of the northern writers began a tradition that passed to other parts of Europe, to bear such exquisite fruit as Dante's *Divine Comedy* and Petrarch's love sonnets. Moreover, the growing devotion to *Notre Dame*—Our Lady—provided a shelter for tender and compassionate love. Our Lady was not terribly logical; she was not so stern as her regal son in enforcing laws. She opened her arms and her heart to little people like the unlettered hero of *Our Lady's Tumbler.* He could not meet the requirements set forth by logic and the law, but he could win her favor with gymnastics and a humble and generous heart.

Still, logic and law seem to surpass love in the thirteenth century. The monasteries declined in influence and prestige as the years passed, partly because of the moral deterioration that seemed inevitably to overtake monasteries after the first hot enthusiasm of the founders, partly because the new towns and courts replaced monasteries as the cultural centers of Europe. The love poetry of the courts suffered too. In the early part of the century, troubadours became fugitives when the crusade against the Albigensians devastated their homeland in southern France. Although France's universities continued to be the best in Europe, the best poetry was soon being written in Italy. And even among the poets and their audiences, a growing cynicism seemed to tarnish the first bright vision of love. Guillaume de Lorris began the *Romance of the Rose* in the first part of the thirteenth century; it was an allegorical poem on love.

When Jean de Meun finished it in the second half of the century, it was a cynical evocation of sensuality.

And the simpler devotees of love did not fare well in the thirteenth century. The followers of Peter Waldo, the merchant of Lyons who had taken up a life of poverty as portrayed in the gospels, found themselves in opposition to the organized Church and were condemned as heretics. St. Francis of Assisi, whose loving heart reached out not only to God and man, but to birds and wolves, to the sun and the moon—St. Francis remained in the good graces of the hierarchy, but he was no less a victim of law and logic. He had hoped that his followers would live lives of simple and unlettered poverty, but their numbers finally forced them to own property in common and to subject their lives to rules and regulations. And not long after Francis' death in 1226, Franciscan friars flocked to the universities to master the logic and the laws of philosophy and theology. These changing prospects, then, make it difficult to generalize about the "twelfth century."

But the hardest generalization to defend is *love* itself. Unlike the other terms, it is not restricted in time or place. Unless twelfth-century people used the word in ways utterly different from one another, unless it meant something then which it no longer means, its definition must include the many forms of love in twelfth-century France, and it must span the eight hundred years which lie between the people of that day and ourselves. Is there any hope of finding some common meaning in the varieties of love? I doubt it. Perhaps the best that we can do is this: *love is a unifying relationship which is appropriate to the things being united.*

This definition would need defending before any western audience, be it twelfth-century or twentieth, since we are accustomed to thinking of love as something existing within an individual—an instinct, an emotion, an attitude—rather than a relationship. Moreover, we commonly and conveniently use love for any one of the emotions associated with the unifying relationship which is love itself. But desire, benevolence, joy, jealousy, tranquility, and anxiety are all attendant to love. No one of them is essential. Love itself is the relationship, begun when the lover first becomes aware of the beloved and progressing through the many forms and degrees experienced by lovers. I love someone when I enter into this relationship; I grow in love when the unifying relationship becomes deeper and stronger.

The definition will also seem odd to many because it can be applied to inanimate objects. But there have been many western thinkers who have thought of love in this all-inclusive way. The solar system, the wolfpack, and the atom find their appropriate unifying relationships spontaneously, without thought or consternation. These patterns of unifying relationships were called love by Boethius. The theme was reaffirmed by the ninth-century philosopher Scotus Erigena: "Love is the connection and bond by which the totality of all things is joined together in ineffable friendship and in indissoluble unity."[1] It was adopted by some of the schoolmen of the twelfth century. It has made its way into the twentieth century in the works of Sigmund Freud, who identified Eros as the power that "holds together everything in the world."[2]

But ordinarily, when we speak of love, we speak of man, and here the question becomes much more difficult. What is the unifying relationship appropriate for man? The presence of man eliminates the simple determinism which seems to rule the universe, and introduces the possibility of moral freedom, of intelligent choice. Unlike atomic particles and protozoa, man is faced with a wide range of possible relationships, and man's experience tells him that the unifying relationships appropriate for himself and his fellow man are discovered, realized, and preserved only with the greatest difficulty.

Simple spontaneity serves nature well, but not man. Nature can afford to be indifferent to the survival of individuals and sometimes even of a whole species, for she will never exhaust her many forms of life. Seemingly without thought, she creates an infinite variety of organisms, well or ill-equipped to survive, endows them with an excess of reproductive energy, and leaves them indifferently to survive or die. But man resists. Individually and collectively, man refuses to be merely one more form of life thrown out and then forgotten by the prodigality of nature. From the very beginning, man learned he must distrust the instincts given him by nature. The Judeo-Christian Adam and the Freudian primal father discovered alike that the man who indulges his taste for pleasure without restraint suffers death as a consequence. From cradle to grave, he either controls his instincts or suffers the penalties inflicted by parents, society, and the universe. In order to survive, a man needs society; therefore, his appetites must be regulated, so that his pursuit of pleasure does not infringe upon another's. Siblings compete with each other and with their father for their mother's attention; rival suitors compete for their beloved's affection; everyone competes for wealth, which brings pleasure and security. If men and women did not agree to master and regulate these competing instincts, they would destroy their society and themselves. Those incapable of accepting restraint are destroyed or imprisoned by society for its own protection.

Furthermore, the peculiarity of man is that his self and therefore the relationships appropriate to himself are never static. They are always changing and fraught with discord, for within man and within human society, the winds blow one way and then another, creating instability, tension, and conflict. Are the winds the flesh versus the spirit, the devil versus God, original sin versus divine grace, good versus evil? Are they the libido versus the super-ego, the life-instinct versus the death-instinct? Whatever they are, man alone must understand the physical, biological, and psychic forces operating within himself and within others and must then devise and achieve the appropriate unifying relationships. Only for man do hatred and moral evil exist. Only for man is love so difficult.

137

So, what kind of relationships are appropriate to man? They must be based on what he is. He needs food, clothing, and shelter. The species must continue, so there must be reproduction. The young must be taught through a process much longer than the education of any other creature. Within the few years of childhood, young humans must learn the contents of a culture which has been millennia in the making. As they grow older, human beings must cooperate in larger and larger groups, in social and political patterns of great complexity. At the same time, their bisexuality leads them to pair off not only for reproduction, but for the physical and psychic satisfaction derived from the complementary nature of the sexes.

Man's needs go beyond this simple list. Man must understand himself. He is conscious that he exists in time and space—that once he did not exist and that one day he will die. He does not accept these facts easily in thought or in feeling; he must look further to find some wider significance for his momentary existence. Perhaps this is the root of man's desire for love and knowledge: his existence is extended through relationships with other parts of reality, it is confirmed through the knowledge of those relationships. In any case, the unifying relationships appropriate for man must include his need to understand.

Moreover, man needs to play. One student of this need, Roger Caillois, has listed the four "principles of play" as competition, chance, simulation, and "vertigo."[3] Hence, relationships appropriate to man must enable him to indulge with control his taste for competition, for gambling, for mimicry, and for disrupted sensory perception.

Small wonder, then, that love means so many things. How many relationships are appropriate to this protean creature man, with his many gifts, his varied appetites, and his changing moods! And how varied are the judgments about what is appropriate and what is not!

Certainly the simplest form of relationship for man is that between himself and non-human creation. For some twelfth-century people, the Albigensians or Cathari, all matter was evil. It could not be loved; there could be no appropriate unifying relationship; one could only yearn to escape the unholy union of the spirit with matter. For most, though, the rest of creation was for the use of man. A knight loved his home, his dinner, his horse; if any of them displeased him, he found another. For the monk, food, drink, and comfort were much less useful since they distracted him from his spiritual home. Therefore, he avoided them. The world was there for the well-being of man; to that all agreed. There was merely divergence over the kind of "well-being" to be pursued, whether it be survival, pleasure, luxury, or salvation—or, most often, some kind of ambiguous mixture.

In more sensitive hearts, the material universe was there not only to be used, but to be revered. They believed that in the beauty and order of creation one could discern the beauty and order of the creator. This belief could be formulated by philosophers, or it could be the more intuitive judgment of a man like Saint

Bruno, founder of the Carthusians, who spoke of "the plain stretching grandly between the mountains, the green fields and flowering pastures, the gently rising line of hills, and the retreats of hidden valleys."[4]

More difficult, though, was the love between persons. The commandments to love God above all things and one's neighbor as oneself placed the love between persons on another level, a more complex level. One could not use God nor fellow-humans as one used an object. Another person was equal to oneself in rationality, in freedom, in self-consciousness, and in immortality. Even love between God and man was based on a kind of equality. St. Bernard wrote, "Of all the movements, feelings, and affections of the soul, love alone enables the creature to answer his creator, responding to him, if not equally, at least in kind."[5]

The kind of love most suited to two persons can be called *reciprocal* interpersonal love, while its less perfect and less complete form can be called *unilateral* interpersonal love. Reciprocal love is a relationship of mutual benevolence and desire between two persons. In this relationship, each person finds pleasure in showing his benevolence toward the other, and each desires and enjoys the benevolence of the other toward himself. In brief, interpersonal love requires giving and taking on the part of both. It is essentially a *shared* experience. It is truly an interpersonal relationship because both persons are consciously participating in the relationship. It can be temporary and superficial, such as friendship between casual acquaintances, or it can be enduring and profound, such as love between a devoted husband and wife.

In manifesting either the giving or the taking attitude, one can be either active or passive. In real reciprocal love, the relationship is a fluctuating one in which each person is alternately giving and taking, active and passive. This fluid character of reciprocal love could be exemplified by describing sexual lovemaking, but describing a conversation between friends serves just as well. When one consoles, instructs, or amuses another, he exemplifies an active giving attitude while the listener exemplifies a passive taking attitude. When a friend speaks, though, to relieve his own mind, to clarify his own thinking, or to take delight in the sound of his own voice, he exemplifies an active taking attitude, while his patient friend exemplifies a passive giving attitude. There can be no reciprocal love when one gives or takes exclusively, and a wholly active or wholly passive individual is inconceivable. In reciprocal interpersonal love, all four attitudes are present in a constantly fluctuating combination.

Unilateral love lacks reciprocity. A person is benevolent toward another (giving) or desires another's benevolence (taking), but because of choice, ignorance, or circumstance, the other person does not respond. Or a person may be benevolent to so many people, all mankind perhaps, that it is impossible for them to respond. Influenced by the Christian and pagan writers of antiquity, twelfth-century thinkers were sometimes inclined to accept unilateral love as an adequate form of love. Too often, they thought of love as a virtue or emotion contained entirely within the individual. Following St. Augustine, they sometimes thought of

God's love for man as God's unilateral benevolence, neglecting their God's obvious interest in being loved in return. They sometimes thought that man's love for God was unilateral desire, neglecting their own generous impulses to give God something in return, an impulse manifested in worship, in sacrifice, and in good works. Poets sometimes stressed the desire of the lover for the beloved, neglecting the implicit inadequacy of a love which is not returned. But in each case, there was something lacking, the element of conscious sharing, of deliberate reciprocity. Unilateral love seems unavoidable in human experience, but it also seems incomplete, an imperfect version of reciprocal love, forced upon us by the inherent limitations of human nature.

If there was a twelfth-century paradigm of interpersonal love, it was the Trinity. For within the Trinity, three persons loved one another with such an intensity that they were one in substance and in nature. At the same time, each person retained his own individuality, complementing the individuality of the other two. It was a love in which each person was giving and taking, a perfect love uniting three faultless persons within a divine union of infinite and everlasting joy. The mystery of the Trinity, which seems so remote to modern man, was an expression of the mystery of love, love which makes one out of many.

But twelfth-century thinkers quarrelled constantly about the Trinity. Small wonder, then, that they could not agree on the nature of love when concrete, imperfect mortals entered the relationship. They were looking for the kinds of unifying relationship appropriate for man, but the variables were too many. Their searches usually came to rest with some incomplete, imperfect version of interpersonal love, whether it be love between God and man, between man and woman, or between man and his fellow man.

The reciprocal love between God and man was the special province of the monks. The reader who believes in the existence of a personal God will accept the possibility of interpersonal love between God and man. But even the atheist should not overlook the experience which Freud called the "oceanic feeling," the feeling of oneness with the totality of being.[6] What is more, the attribution of personal characteristics to the fundamental principle of the universe is not necessarily foreign to the atheist who has experienced human love, for human lovers commonly attribute qualities to their beloveds which the beloveds do not obviously possess. After speaking of love among human beings, Erich Fromm says that "the religious form of love, that which is called the love of God, is, psychologically speaking, not different."[7] The monastic attempt to achieve the appropriate unifying relationship with God may then be instructive even for the nonbeliever.

The monk's life was ordered to achieving and understanding interpersonal love with God. Like all men, he learned soon after birth that in the struggle to survive, he was forced to play the unwilling mediator between the external universe and his internal instincts, both of which seemed to propel him toward extinction. His

Christian beliefs called upon him to transcend both and to seek an immaterial God. For what was man's fundamental need? Life. What a fragile grip he had on that one precious possession! The tenuously living creature looked to God, the source of life, for sustenance, and God responded with the promise of eternal life. He manifested himself in the power and order and beauty of the universe; and as an even greater concession to human frailty, he became man and walked the earth. In the New Testament, the monk found God in human form curing the ill, feeding the hungry, raising the dead, and in a final dramatic victory over death, dying himself, only to rise again. In Jesus' humanity, the monk found a human being capable of understanding and responding to other human beings. In Jesus' divinity, he found an infinite God who could know and love each man individually, not impeded in the slightest by the sheer numbers of those to be loved. Jesus was a cosmic detour in which God went out of his way to offer man life and love.

But how could man return God's benevolence? It seemed blasphemous to say God needed man's benevolence, but he certainly seemed to expect it and man was certainly free to refuse it. The first commandment was to love God, to enter wholeheartedly into this interpersonal relationship with him. To do so, the monk was inclined to reject his own nature. God was spiritual, man was weighted down by matter, so man must spiritualize himself through asceticism. He must make himself indifferent to his material surroundings and reduce his bodily appetites to submission. Thus spiritualized, he could approach his immaterial God. The monks knew the doctrine of the resurrection of the body, that their souls would ultimately be rejoined with their bodies, but they could only expect that their bodies would be spiritualized in a way appropriate for a union with a spiritual God. In the meantime, the body was an embarrassment, not necessarily condemned, but certainly suspect. It was hard to fit the body into the unifying relationship with God.

Despite their suspicion of man's material constitution, though, the monks did integrate some of man's fundamental emotions into their form of love. Guilt, which all experience, was channelled partly into aggression against self in penitential practices, but more successfully into remorse and appeals for forgiveness. The "gift of tears," through which man felt the full impact of his failings, was much treasured by the monks, because it enabled them then to experience with equal force the relief of God's forgiveness. From the depths of guilt they rose to the heights of God's love and forgiveness, a psychic liberation of no slight significance. Moreover, if Freud is correct in believing that affection arises from inhibition of the sexual drive, that it is "aim-inhibited love," then the celibacy of the conscientious monk enabled him to channel all his libidinal energy into the emotional bond with God. The liberating experience of repentance and forgiveness was intensified and directed toward God by the careful control of sexual instincts.

The Freudian utopians Norman Brown and Herbert Marcuse have rejected repression, sublimation, and aim-inhabition as valid ways to live a satisfactory human life. And surely no monk expected to reach in this life the goal described by Marcuse: "the universal gratification of the basic human needs, and the freedom from guilt and fear—internalized as well as external, instinctual as well as 'rational.'"[8] But the monks' hope to achieve it in another life was sustained by the very real progess they experienced in this world. They rejected erotic pleasure as an acceptable form of human experience, and they were slow to apply their theories to love between humans, but they harnessed sexual energies in their loving relationship with God. Their theories were based on an excessively spiritualized conception of the human person, but in practice, they understood better than anyone else that the appropriate unifying relationship between persons was the elusive product of sustained effort, of the careful and determined engineering of all the resources of the human person.

Like the monks, the courtly poets were authorities on reciprocal love between persons. Their understanding of the human person, male and female, made them no less contemptuous than the monks of the rapist's animal lust and of the seducer's diabolic deception. But the poets went further. That man and woman should come together in sexual union was obvious to almost everyone. That they should bring forth children was equally obvious. That they should take pleasure in their union seems obvious now, but in the world of Christian ascetics, it was denied. Surely among the boldest thinkers of the century, the poets affirmed the value of shared erotic experience. What is more, they went beyond the simple fact of physical pleasure and explored the psychic currents of erotic love. The appropriate unifying relationship between a man and a woman was not merely attraction between two souls or between two bodies but was a fluctuating current between two whole personalities. It was all lust to more conventional thinkers, but the poets refined desire and found among the baser minerals the glittering substance of interpersonal erotic love.

The poets also integrated this discovery with man's need to play. Their poetry made romantic love into a game of great fascination. It had the prime ingredient of sexual excitement. It was a game of chance, in that both love and lovers were fickle, and no amount of information would enable one to predict where Cupid's darts would fall. It was competitive, since suitors vied for a lady's attention, doing deeds of valor and courtesy to win her favor. It involved what Caillois calls "vertigo," the disruption of ordinary sense perception, for lovers fasted and grew pale, they became insensible to everything but their love, they grew faint and swooned, and they did all this in an aura of sexual excitement.

And as the rules of courtesy became more formalized, romantic love took on more characteristics of a game. Courtly behavior became a kind of ritual in which each played a part, a kind of mimicry. And, most important for a game, its field was circumscribed in time and place, sheltered by the imagination from harsh social realities, played according to rules less

147

complicated than the rules of real life. The valid insights of the poets could not be integrated into twelfth-century life, but they were preserved in the play of aristocratic culture. And even in the game itself, one finds an understanding of human needs lacking in the severity of the monks.

The isolation of erotic love in time and space was unfortunate. The poets surely knew that in describing early forms of love they had not completely presented the appropriate unifying relationship between man and woman. They had discovered something, but they did not pursue their discovery with the persistence of the monks nor with the breadth of vision of the schoolmen. They had achieved new insights into the appropriate unifying relationship between man and woman, but their searching stopped at the end of the poem, at the end of the game. So they had nothing to say about how the relationship between man and woman changes over extended time, how it is modified by the birth of children, how individual characteristics, so deeply rooted as to be immovable, persevere to the end as sources of consolation and irritation to the other, and how the process of revelation and discovery leads to the growth and psychic intertwining of two imperfect personalities. In brief, the poets did not discover conjugal love.

But then, neither did anyone else. The schoolmen had little to say about reciprocal love. When they described the appropriate unifying relationship between man and woman, they took into account the needs of society, but they saw husband and wife almost as celibates who had children. In the minds of the clergy, the ideal parents were like affectionate brother and sister, except that they copulated to have children and to relieve lustful desires in the way least damaging to themselves and to society. Like modern sociologists, the schoolmen insisted that man's sexual instincts must be controlled so that they serve society. The instincts should not work violence on others through rape; they should not take what is another's through adultery; they should not be indulged at the expense of the offspring they create. The schoolmen were sensible. What they said was good for society. It was good for individuals too, in so far as it defended the worth of every person and insisted that marriage was up to the free choice of the individual. But because they thought of love as a virtue or affection inhering in the individual, they neglected the experience of reciprocal interpersonal love, and, because of their condemnation of erotic pleasure, the schoolmen offered nothing about conjugal love, the most complex, the most variable, and the most profound form of interpersonal love among humans.

Knights looked for appropriate unifying relationships too, but for them nearly all relationships were questions of power: lord and vassal, husband and wife, parent and child. The fundamental thrust of the Christian commandment to love one's neighbor as one's self was egalitarian, but nothing was more foreign to the hierarchical mentality of French knights than this egalitarian sentiment. Men were equal in the eyes of God, but not in the eyes of one another. A knight was stronger than a serf, a man was stronger than a woman. The appropriate unifying relationship was sought in the light of this disparity of power, not in the light of the egalitarian commandment to love others as one's self. Just as Roland loved his friend Oliver, knights were more inclined to love their fellow warriors than anyone else.[9] When schoolmen made the free consent of the woman a necessary ingredient for marriage, when courtly poets exalted women above knights, they were trying to correct the power-ethic of the knights. Neither schoolmen nor poets changed the basic structure of society, but their combined efforts did modify courtly notions about the appropriate relationships between man and woman.

Love between man and woman was a special form of love between human beings. The more general question, of the appropriate unifying relationship between human beings, was equally difficult. The fundamental dilemma was inherent in human nature: man can only attend to one thing at a time. The time given to one friend cannot be given to another. An hour spent praying cannot be spent playing with one's children. Time spent feeding the poor is not available for tending the sick. To embrace one woman is to turn away from many others. "The unmarried man is anxious about the affairs of the Lord, how to please the Lord; but the married man is anxious about worldly affairs, how to please his wife, and his interests are divided" (I Cor.7:32–33). What, then, are the unifying relationships appropriate among men?

Only the most severe of the monks, like Arnulf of

Boyers (see p. 68), had a simple answer to this question. They rejected any form of reciprocal love among humans. Each monk was to show all men equal and unilateral benevolence. This was, they thought, how God loved man. But unlike God, man should not desire or expect any special love in return. This answer was simple and self-effacing. It made love an impersonal and unilateral benevolence, uncomplicated by personal interactions. And the practice of avoiding other human beings as much as possible made it all the easier to be impersonal and benevolent. One merely prayed for all mankind.

Most others, though, struggled with the problem without resolving it, for it cannot really be resolved. Unilateral love—wishing others well, preaching the gospel, giving alms to the poor, protecting widows and orphans—was praised by all as the most obvious way to love one's neighbor. After all, the good Samaritan had shown only unilateral benevolence. According to the parable, he looked after the man who had been beaten without so much as asking his name. But even this form of love of neighbor distracted one from thinking about God. When Martha complained that her sister neglected her work of serving others to sit at the feet of Jesus, Jesus said, "Martha, Martha, you are anxious and troubled about many things; one thing is needful. Mary has chosen the best part, which shall not be taken away from her" (Luke 10:41–42). Twelfth-century thinkers did not resolve the dilemma of Mary and Martha. Bernard himself left the cloister to look after the needs of Christendom but then felt guilty for having done so. Conversely, he discouraged the arch-bishop of York from becoming a monk because he would thereby deprive his archdiocese of his loving care.[10]

The problem was to find a balance among the different kinds of love. Each man should achieve a reciprocal love with God. He could hope to achieve a reciprocal love with a few friends, but certainly not with the vast majority of his fellow men. He could achieve an erotic interpersonal love with one woman. But if there were more, love was shallow and transitory. He could try to extend unilateral love to all mankind, but in practice the very demands of love in the service of some required him to turn his back on others. The limitations of human nature required man to choose among or to balance all these needs and obligations, to accept the tension among them, to try to maintain some kind of equilibrium, and to live with the inadequacy of his efforts.

This equilibrium—the schoolmen would call it "ordered love"—was not maintained perfectly by anyone, and the thinkers of the day were quick to point out imbalances in the love-lives of others. Preachers condemned the imbalance as sin and satirists laughed at it as folly. Impersonal lust was condemned by monks and schoolmen alike as unworthy of man and offensive to God. The poets merely distinguished reciprocal erotic love from impersonal lust, which they too considered inordinate. Andreas Capellanus ridiculed the hypocrisy of courtiers who pretended to seek true interpersonal erotic love ("pure love") but who were in fact playing the game of seduction, but he was equally sardonic in presenting the unbalanced and misogynous ravings of other worldly clerics and monks. Others told the ribald stories in which women and clerics abandoned the forms of love to which they had pledged themselves for the sake of avarice, lust, and hypocrisy. The failures of twelfth-century lovers were well known at the time.

No one in the twelfth century achieved the equilibrium in practice; no one achieved it in theory. That is to say, no one put together the ideas of contemporaries into a comprehensive theory of love, incorporating all its forms, and no one realized in his own life a perfect balance of the demands of nature and of God. For that failure we can blame in part the strong traditions, derived mainly from Plato and St. Paul, which sharply divided the human being into body and soul. No theory based on those traditions could be completely true to human experience. We can blame in part the tradition of thinking of love as an individual act independent of the beloved. But we must also blame the inherent limitations of human nature, limitations as restrictive today as they were then.

Of course, people could pretend that the limitations were not there. Some fastened on only one of the competing demands of reality as though it were everything. Like the courtly poets who spoke only of incipient erotic love, one could indulge in a "truancy, alike from vulgar common sense and from the ten commandments,"[11] but it was hard to sustain that kind of myopia. A remarkable number of troubadours ended their days in monasteries.[12] Many others no doubt took the broad view but deluded themselves into thinking that they had achieved the equilibrium, that they had in fact met the requirements of human nature and of the gospel. They were the complacent, the self-righteous. Others placed themselves above the problem, playing the role of the witty cynic. They did not pursue love because there was no love to pursue; it was merely a ruse for obtaining more tangible benefits, like money or sexual pleasure. The cynic and the hypocrite will always view each other with contempt, but they are one in their self-righteousness.

But the best of twelfth-century people struggled after love and met success and failure intermixed. Like modern man's, their achievements were limited by the narrowness of their understanding, by the inconstancy of their spirits, by the harsh demands of a society seeking its own survival, and by the vagaries of fortune. Whatever love they experienced was bittersweet, because it always fell short of love in its perfection, love in which all things would find their appropriate unifying relationships, in which God and man, man and woman, man and fellow-man would realize a warm and deep and everlasting communion. The vision of that love was described by Hugh of St. Victor, speaking of the love which God offered man:

That love is unique but not private, alone but not isolated, shared but not divided, both communal and individual, a singular love of all and a total love of each, not decreased by sharing nor diminished by use; not aging in time, ever old, ever new; desirable to anticipate, sweet to experience, eternal in its fruits, full of delight, restoring and satisfying, never growing tiresome.[13]

That was the ideal pursued by the lovers of twelfth-century France. They did not find it in this world, but perhaps they found it where Abelard said they would, in that True Jerusalem:

> That city where unending peace
> And faultless joy shall reign,
> Where yearning meets the yearned for,
> Where longing's not in vain.

> *Vera Jerusalem*
> *est illa civitas*
> *cujus pax jugis est,*
> *summa iucunditas:*
> *ubi non praevenit*
> *rem desiderium,*
> *nec desiderio*
> *minus est praemium.*[14]

Notes

NOTES TO CHAPTER ONE

1. *Tractatus de quatuor gradibus violentiae charitatis*, PL, 196:1207.

2. Albert Blaise, *Dictionnaire latin-française des auteurs chrétiens* (Turnhout, Belgium, 1954); Hélène Pétré, *Caritas: Etude sur le vocabulaire latin de la charité chrétienne* (Louvain, 1948); Walther von Wartburg, *Französisches Etymologisches Wörterbuch*, 2 (Leipsig and Berlin, 1940), 376–77.

3. Andreas Capellanus, *The Art of Courtly Love*, trans. John J. Parry (New York, 1959), p. 171.

4. *The Letters of St. Bernard of Clairvaux*, trans. Bruno James (Chicago, 1953), p. 388.

5. *Ex libro III historiae regum Francorum*, RHGF, 12:219.

6. *Cligés*, trans. W. W. Comfort, in *Arthurian Romances* (London and New York, 1965), p. 91.

7. *Ex chronico Mauriniacensi*, RHGF, 12:80.

8. *The Letters of Peter the Venerable*, ed. Giles Constable (Cambridge, Mass., 1967), 1:145.

9. *Letters*, trans. James, p. 402.

10. *Ibid.*, p. 325.

11. *Ex chronico S. Petri Vivi Senonensis*, RHGF, 12:282.

12. *Fragmentum historiae ex veteri membrana de tributo Floriacensibus imposito*, RHGF, 12:94.

13. *Ex chronico Mauriniacensi,* RHGF, 12:72.

14. *Historia gloriosa regis Ludovici VII,* RHGF, 12:131.

15. Achille Luchaire, *Social France at the Time of Philip Augustus,* trans. E. B. Krehbiel, introd. by John W. Baldwin (New York, 1967), p. 15.

NOTES TO CHAPTER TWO

1. Macrobius, *Commentary on the Dream of Scipio,* trans. William Harris Stahl (New York, 1952), p. 245.

2. *The Confessions of Saint Augustine,* trans. Edward B. Pusey (New York, 1949), p. 24.

3. *Ibid.,* p. 30.

4. Trans. Cuthbert Butler in *Benedictine Monachism* (Cambridge and New York, 1961), p. 86.

5. *Confessions,* pp. 145, 169–70.

6. Trans. Karl F. Morrison, *Rome and the City of God* (Philadelphia, 1964), pp. 46–47.

7. *The City of God,* trans. Marcus Dods (New York, 1950), pp. 481 (XV. 3), 684–85 (XIX. 8); *Confessions,* p. 30.

8. PL, 16:190–94.

9. PL, 22:335, Letter III.

10. *Select Letters of St. Jerome,* ed. and trans. F. A. Wright (London and Cambridge, Mass., 1933), p. 183, Letter XLV, to Asella.

11. *Collatio decima sexta: De amicitia,* PL, 49:1011–44.

12. *Ibid.,* col. 1019.

13. Trans. Owen Chadwick, *John Cassian: A Study in Primitive Monasticism,* 1st ed. (Cambridge, 1950), pp. 105–6.

14. Trans. Butler, *Benedictine Monachism,* p. 85.

NOTES TO CHAPTER THREE

1. *Epistola ad Fratres de Monte Dei,* PL, 184:313–14.

2. G. G. Coulton, *Five Centuries of Religion,* 1, 2nd ed. (Cambridge, 1929), 255.

3. Peter Dronke, *Medieval Latin and the Rise of the European Love-Lyric,* 2nd ed. (Oxford, 1968), 1:213–19.

4. Quoted by Jean Leclercq, *The Love of Learning and the Desire for God,* trans. Catharine Misrahi (New York, 1961), p. 316.

5. *De diligendo Deo,* PL, 182:973–1000. The column references in the following discussion all refer to this edition.

6. *De contemplando Deo,* PL, 184:365–80; *De natura et dignitate amoris,* PL, 184:379–407; *Epistola ad Fratres de Monte Dei,* PL, 184:307–54.

7. *Epistola,* PL, 184:309.

8. *De natura,* PL, 184:396.

9. *Epistola,* PL, 184:336.

10. *Ibid.,* col. 335.

11. *De natura,* PL, 184:382, 390–92.

12. *Epistola,* PL, 184:315–17.

13. *De natura,* PL, 184:399.

14. *Ibid.,* cols. 397–98 (quotation), 408.

15. *Epistola,* PL, 184:339.

16. *De natura,* PL, 184:403.

17. *Epistola,* PL, 184:352.

18. *Ibid.,* col. 349.

19. See Francis Wenner, "Charité," *Dictionnaire de spiritualité,* 2 (Paris, 1953), 571–72.

20. Ailred of Rievaulx, *Mirror of Charity,* trans. Geoffrey Webb and Adrian Walker (London, 1962), p. 92.

21. PL, 184:11–252.

22. *Letters,* ed. James, pp. 136, 243–45.

23. Trans. Coulton, *Five Centuries,* 1:301.

24. *Meditations of Guigo, Prior of the Charterhouse,* trans. John Jolin (Milwaukee, 1951), pp. 25, 49.

25. *Letters,* trans. James, p. 139.

26. *Ibid.,* pp. 407–8.

27. PL, 183:909.

28. E. Vansteenberghe, "Deux théoriciens de l'amitié au XIIe siecle, Pierre de Blois et Aelred de Riéval," *Revue des sciences religieuses,* 12 (1932), 572–88.

29. *De spirituale amicitia,* PL, 195:659–701; quote, col. 679. The column numbers in the following discussion all refer to this edition.

30. See *Letters,* trans. James, pp. 183, 514.

31. *Sermones in Cantica Canticorum,* PL, 183:807.

32. *Letters,* ed. Constable, 1:307–8

158

NOTES TO CHAPTER FOUR

1. *Ex chronico Mauriniacensi*, RHGF, 12:88.

2. *Historia gloriosa regis Ludovici VII*, RHGF, 12:133.

3. Trans. W. S. Merwin in *Medieval Epics* (New York, 1963), pp. 132–33. © 1963 by Random House.

4. Trans. Muriel Kittel in *Medieval Age*, ed. Angel Flores (New York, 1963), pp. 173–74.

5. Works exemplifying these interpretations are: literary influences: Irénée Cluzel, "Quelques réflexions à propos des origines de la poésie lyrique des troubadours," *Cahiers de civilisation médiévale*, 4 (1961), 179–88; influence of women: Sidney Painter, *French Chivalry* (Ithaca, 1961), Myrrha Lot-Borodine, *De l'amour profane à l'amour sacré* (Paris, 1961), René Nelli, *L'érotique des troubadours* (Toulouse, 1963); sex ratio: Herbert Moller, "The Social Causation of the Courtly Love Complex," *Comparative Studies in Society and History*, 1 (1959), 137–63; psychological state of the poets: Herbert Moller, "The Meaning of Courtly Love," *Journal of American Folklore*, 73 (1960), 39–52, Maurice Valency, *In Praise of Love* (New York, 1958), p. 32; influence of heresy: A. J. Denomy, *The Heresy of Courtly Love* (New York, 1947).

6. Valency, *In Praise of Love*, p. 143.

7. Trans. Harvey Birenbaum in *Medieval Age*, ed. Flores, pp. 180–81.

8. These stories can be found in *Lays of Marie de France*, trans. Eugene Mason (London and New York, 1964).

9. The page references that follow are to Chrétien de Troyes, *Arthurian Romances*, trans. Comfort.

10. Trans. Jack Lindsay in *Medieval Age*, ed. Flores, p. 182.

11. Trans. James J. Wilhelm, *ibid.*, pp. 186–87.

NOTES TO CHAPTER FIVE

1. *Ex chronico Mauriniacensi*, RHGF, 12:81.

2. *Self and Society in Medieval France: The Memoirs of Abbot Guibert of Nogent*, trans. C. C. Swinton Bland, ed. with introduction by John F. Benton (New York and Evanston, 1970), pp. 173–90.

3. *Ex brevi chronico S. Martini Turonensis*, RHGF, 12:65.

4. *Historia gloriosa regis Ludovici VII,* RHGF, 12:126.

5. *Ibid., p. 132.*

6. *Adam, a Religious Play of the Twelfth Century,* trans. from Norman French and Latin by Edward Noble Stone (Seattle, 1926).

7. *Fabliaux,* trans. Robert Hellman and Richard O'Gorman (New York, 1965), pp. 1–16. Per Nykrog has argued effectively that the fabliaux were not "bourgeois" in the sense that they were written by and for bourgeoisie (*Les fabliaux: étude d'histoire littéraire et de stylistique médiévale* [Copenhagen, 1957]), but I still think it likely that townsmen provided an appreciative audience.

8. *Ex anonymi chronico,* RHGF, 12:120.

9. *The Didascalicon of Hugh of St. Victor,* trans. Jeremy Taylor (New York and London, 1961), p. 137.

10. PL, 192:816–17.

11. *Sentences,* PL, 192:812–14, 821–22.

12. *Liber de planctu naturae,* PL, 210:447.

13. *De laude charitatis,* PL, 176:974.

14. *Liber de planctu naturae,* PL, 210:447.

15. Ernst Curtius, *European Literature and the Latin Middle Ages,* trans. Willard R. Trask (New York and Evanston, 1963), p. 112.

16. *Sententiae,* PL, 192:818–19.

17. For example, Peter Lombard, *Sententiae,* PL, 192:920; Alain of Lille, *Summa de arte praedicatoria,* PL, 210:193–94.

18. *De Trinitate,* PL, 196:965.

19. *Tractatus de quatuor gradibus violentiae charitatis,* PL, 196:1207–24.

20. *Ibid.,* col. 1214.

21. Quoted by Etienne Gilson, *Heloise and Abelard,* trans. L. K. Shook (Ann Arbor, 1960), p. 33.

22. *The Letters of Abelard and Heloise,* trans. C. K. Scott Moncrieff (New York, 1942), pp. 81–82.

23. Curtius, *European Literature,* p. 414.

24. *Ibid.,* pp. 113–17.

25. Trans. Muriel Kittel in *Medieval Age,* ed. Flores, p. 158.

26. *Mediaeval Latin Lyrics,* trans. Helen Waddell, 5th ed. (London, 1948), pp. 173–74.

27. "Das Liebesconcil," ed. G. Waitz, *Zeitschrift für Deutsches Altertum,* 7 (1849), 160–67.

28. Trans. as *The Art of Courtly Love* by John J. Parry (New York, 1959). Further page references are to this edition.

NOTES TO CHAPTER SIX

1. Quoted by Richard H. Green, "Alan of Lille's *De Planctu Naturae,*" *Speculum,* 31 (1956), 666, n. 37.

2. Quoted by Herbert Marcuse, *Eros and Civilization* (New York: Vintage, n.d.), pp. 38–39.

3. Roger Caillois, *Man, Play, and Games,* trans. Meyer Barash (New York, 1961), pp. 11–35.

4. Quoted by L. Genicot, *La spiritualité médiévale* (Paris, 1958), p. 49.

5. *Sermones in Cantica,* PL, 183:1183.

6. Sigmund Freud, *Civilization and Its Discontents,* trans. James Strachey (New York, 1962), p. 19.

7. *The Art of Loving* (New York, 1956), p. 63.

8. Marcuse, *Eros and Civilization,* p. 139.

9. See Nelli, *L'érotique des troubadours,* pp. 277–325.

10. *Letters,* trans. James, pp. 244–45.

11. C. S. Lewis, *The Allegory of Love* (New York, 1958), p. 172.

12. Jean Boutière and A. H. Schutz, eds., *Biographies des troubadours,* rev. ed. by Boutière (Paris, 1964), p. 270, n. 10.

13. *Soliloquium de arrha animae,* PL, 176:959.

14. *Mediaeval Latin Lyrics,* ed. Waddell, p. 162.

Bibliographical Note

PRIMARY SOURCES IN TRANSLATION

THE FOLLOWING translations are mainly those that I have cited in this volume. The reader can locate others by consulting the card catalogue of his library and such reference works as Clarissa P. Ferrar and Austin P. Evans, *Bibliography of English Translations from Medieval Sources* (New York, 1946) and *Paperbound Books in Print.*

Works from antiquity: *The Confessions of St. Augustine,* trans. Edward B. Pusey (New York, 1949); St. Augustine's *City of God,* trans. Marcus Dods (New York, 1950); *Selected Letters of St. Jerome,* ed. and trans. F. A. Wright (London and Cambridge, Mass., 1933); and Macrobius, *Commentary on the Dream of Scipio,* trans. William Harris Stahl (New York, 1952).

Monastic authors: *The Letters of St. Bernard of Clairvaux,* trans. Bruno James (Chicago, 1953); *Meditations of Guigo, Prior of the Charterhouse,* trans. John Jolin (Milwaukee, 1951); Ailred of Rievaulx, *Mirror of Charity,* trans. Geoffrey Webb and Adrian Walker (London, 1962). See also the memoirs of Guibert of Nogent, cited below. Two additional translations are *The Book of Saint Bernard on the Love of God,* trans. Edmund G. Gardner (New York, n. d. [1915]) and Ailred's *De spirituale amicitia,* trans. as *Christian Friendship* by C. H. Talbot (London, 1942).

Courtly writers: Chrétien de Troyes, *Arthurian Romances,* trans. W. W. Comfort (London and New York, 1965); *Lays of Marie de France,* trans. Eugene Mason (London and New York, 1964). Anthologies I have cited are *Medieval Epics* (New York, 1963), and *Medieval Age,* ed. Angel Flores (New York, 1963). Wilhelm's book, *Seven Troubadours,* cited below, has a number of poems in translation.

Authors whom I have associated with towns: Self and Society in Medieval France: The Memoirs of Abbot Guibert of Nogent, trans. C. C. Swinton Bland, ed., rev., and introd. by John F. Benton (New York and Evanston, 1970); *Adam, a Religious Play of the Twelfth Century,* trans. Edward Noble Stone (Seattle, 1926); *Fabliaux,* trans. Robert Hellman and Richard O'Gorman (New York, 1965); *The Didascalicon of Hugh of St. Victor,* trans. Jerome Taylor (New York and London, 1961); Alain of Lille, *Complaint of Nature,* trans. Douglas M. Moffat (New York, 1908); *The Letters of Abelard and Heloise,* trans. C. K. Scott Moncrieff (New York, 1942); Andreas Capellanus, *The Art of Courtly Love,* trans. John J. Parry (New York, 1959). Excellent anthologies are *Mediaeval Latin Lyrics,* ed. and trans. Helen Waddell, 5th ed. (London, 1948) and *Heresies of the High Middle Ages,* ed. Walter L. Wakefield (New York, 1969).

SECONDARY WORKS

Good general histories are Georges Duby and Robert Mandrou, *A History of French Civilization,* trans. James B. Adkinson (New York, 1964) and Friedrich Heer, *The Medieval World; Europe: 1100–1350,* trans. Janet Sondheimer (New York, 1963). There are many useful articles and bibliographies in *The New Catholic Encyclopedia,* 15 vols. (New York, 1967).

A sense of what daily life was like in twelfth-century France can be acquired from Achille Luchaire, *Social France at the Time of Philip Augustus,* trans. E. B. Krehbiel, introd. by John W. Baldwin (New York, 1967) and Urban T. Holmes, Jr., *Daily Living in the Twelfth Century* (Madison, Wis., 1964). A superb interpretation of the period is provided by R. W. Southern, *The Making of the Middle Ages* (New Haven, 1961). See also the same author's *Medieval Humanism and Other Studies* (New York and Evanston, 1970). An excellent collection of essays appears in *Twelfth-Century Europe and the Foundations of Modern Society,* ed. Marshall Clagett *et al.* (Madison, Wis., 1966); and a recent work of much value is Christopher Brooke, *The Twelfth Century Renaissance* (New York, 1970).

The twelfth-century inheritance from antiquity can be seen in R. R. Bolgar, *The Classical Heritage and Its Beneficiaries* (Cambridge, 1954); E. K. Rand, *Founders of the Middle Ages* (Cambridge, Mass., 1928) and his *Ovid and His Influence* (Boston, 1925); C. H. Haskins, *The Renaissance of the Twelfth Century* (Cambridge, Mass., 1927); Raymond Klibansky, *The Continuity of the Platonic Tradition during the Middle Ages* (London, 1939); and Joseph Anthony Mazzeo, "Plato's Eros and Dante's Amore," *Traditio,* 12 (1956), 315–37. Antique ideas on love are described in Robert Flacelière, *Love in Ancient Greece,* trans. James Cleugh (New York, 1962); Georg Luck, *The Latin Love Elegy* (New York, 1960); and John Burnaby's excellent *Amor Dei: A Study of the Religion of St. Augustine* (London, 1938). Many of the works listed below contain material on the ancient antecedents of the twelfth century.

For monasticism, see Owen Chadwick, *John Cassian,* 2nd ed. (Cambridge, 1968); Cuthbert Butler, *Benedictine Monachism* (Cambridge and New York, 1961) and the same author's *Western Mysticism,* 2nd ed. (London, 1951); Jean Leclercq, *The Love of Learning and the Desire for God,* trans. Catharine Misrahi (New York, 1961); and Etienne Gilson,

The Mystical Theology of Saint Bernard, trans. A. H. C. Downes (London and New York, 1940). The works of David Knowles provide sympathetic and highly reliable commentaries on medieval monasticism; those of G. G. Coulton are less sympathetic and are out of date, but they are still valuable. Works on individual figures are Watkin Williams, *Saint Bernard of Clairvaux* (Manchester, 1935); J. M. Déchanet, *Guillaume de Saint-Thierry* (Bruges, 1942); and Amédée Hallier, *The Monastic Theology of Aelred of Rievaulx: An Experiential Theology,* trans. Columban Heaney (Spencer, Mass., 1969).

For dynastic history, see Charles Petit-Dutaillis, *The Feudal Monarchy in France and England from the Tenth to the Thirteenth Century,* trans. E. D. Hunt (London, 1936); A. Luchaire, *Les premiers capétiens (987–1137)* (Paris, 1901), part 2 of vol. II of *Histoire de France,* ed. Ernest Lavisse; and *Institutions seigneuriales,* vol. I (Paris, 1957) of *Histoire des institutions françaises au moyen âge,* ed. Ferdinand Lot and Robert Fawtier. A number of useful articles on aristocratic life are in *Lordship and Community in Medieval Europe,* ed. Fredic Cheyette (New York, 1968). The most thorough discussion of aristocratic patronage of literature is Reto R. Bezzola, *Les origines et la formation de la littérature courtoise,* part III: *La société courtoise: Littérature de cour et littérature courtoise,* 2 vols. (Paris, 1963); but see also John F. Benton, "The Court of Champagne as a Literary Center," *Speculum,* 36 (1961), 551–91.

For literature and ideas in general, H. O. Taylor, *The Mediaeval Mind,* 4th ed. 2 vols. (Cambridge, Mass., 1951) is still a good introduction. More specialized works on literature are Ernst Curtius, *European Literature and the Latin Middle Ages,* trans. Willard R. Trask (New York and Evanston, 1963); Urban T. Holmes, Jr., *A History of Old French Literature,* rev. ed. (New York, 1962); and Peter Dronke, *Medieval Latin and the Rise of the European Love-Lyric,* 2nd ed., 2 vols. (Oxford, 1968). The distinctiveness of individual troubadours is emphasized in James J. Wilhelm, *Seven Trou-badours: The Creators of Modern Verse* (University Park and London, 1970).

The place of love in twelfth-century life and literature has been the highly controversial subject of an enormous body of scholarly writing. The best introduction to the controversies over "courtly love" is the editor's preface to *The Meaning of Courtly Love,* ed. F. X. Newman (Albany, 1968). This small volume contains excellent papers by distinguished scholars and a good bibliography. The most readable introduction to the love poetry itself is Maurice Valency, *In Praise of Love* (New York, 1958). The theory that there was a systematic set of beliefs which can be called "courtly love" and which were set forth seriously by Andreas Capellanus has been spread especially by C. S. Lewis, *The Allegory of Love* (New York, 1958; first publ. 1936) and Sidney Painter, *French Chivalry* (Ithaca, 1961, first publ. 1940). This theory has been chal-lenged by a number of scholars who consider Andreas' intent to be satirical but who nevertheless differ considerably among themselves. The most important of these are Durant W. Robertson, Jr., *A Preface to Chaucer* (Princeton, 1963); E. Talbot Donaldson, "The Myth of Courtly Love," *Ventures,* 5, 2 (1965), 16–23; and Peter Dronke, *European Love-Lyric,* cited above.

Life in the towns is described in two works cited above, Holmes, *Daily Living,* and Luchaire, *Social France.* The reflections of Paris masters on moral problems facing towns-people are presented in John W. Baldwin, *Masters, Princes, and Merchants: The Social Views of Peter the Chanter and His Circle,* 2 vols. (Princeton, 1970); but one finds little on love in any of these volumes. For heresies, see Jeffrey Burton Russell, *Dissent and Reform in the Early Middle Ages* (Berke-ley and Los Angeles, 1965).

A good introduction to the intellectual life of the period is David Knowles, *The Evolution of Medieval Thought* (New York, 1964). For the attitudes of schoolmen toward sexuality and marriage, see John T. Noonan, Jr., *Contraception: A History of Its Treatment by the Catholic Theologians and Canonists* (Cambridge, Mass., 1965); the same author's "Marital Affection in the Canonists," *Studia Gratiana,* 12 (1967), 479–509; and the several articles on "Marriage" in the *Dictionnaire de théologie catholique,* 9 (Paris, 1926), 2044–335. Useful works on individual authors are G. Raynaud de Lage, *Alain de Lille* (Montreal and Paris, 1951); Richard H. Green, "Alan of Lille's *De Planctu Naturae,*" *Speculum,* 31 (1956), 649–74; Philippe Delhaye, *Pierre Lombard: Sa vie, ses oeuvres, sa morale* (Montreal and Paris, 1961); Gervais Dumeige, *Richard de Saint-Victor et l'idée chrétienne de l'amour* (Paris, 1952); and Etienne Gilson, *Heloise and Abelard,* trans. L. K. Shook (Ann Arbor, 1960), and Leif Grane, *Heloise and Abelard: Philosophy and Christianity in the Middle Ages,* trans. Frederick and Christine Crowley (New York, 1970). For the less formal lives of students and masters, see Helen Waddell, *The Wandering Scholars,* 6th ed. (Garden City, 1961).

On the thirteenth and fourteenth centuries, see Heer, *The Medieval World,* cited above, and J. Huizinga, *The Waning of the Middle Ages,* trans. F. Hopman (Garden City, 1956).

The best introduction to the general history and philosophy of love is Irving Singer, *The Nature of Love: Plato to Luther* (New York, 1966), with the qualifications expressed in my review of that volume, "The Origins of Western Ideas: Irving Singer's *The Nature of Love: Plato to Luther,*" *Journal of the History of Ideas,* 29 (1968), 141–51. See also the learned and urbane Martin C. D'Arcy, *The Mind and Heart of Love: Lion and Unicorn, a Study in Eros and Agape,* rev. ed. (New York, 1956). For an anthology of readings on love, see *The Idea of Love,* ed. Robert G. Hazo (New York, 1967).

Index